CULTURES OF THE WORLD

CAMBODIA

Sean Sheehan

MARSHALL CAVENDISH
New York • London • Sydney

Reference edition published 1996 by
Marshall Cavendish Corporation
99 White Plains Road
P.O. Box 2001
Tarrytown
New York 10591

© Times Editions Pte Ltd 1996

Originated and designed by
Times Books International, an imprint of
Times Editions Pte Ltd

Printed in Singapore

Library of Congress Cataloging-in-Publication Data:
Sheehan, Sean, 1951-
 Cambodia / Sean Sheehan.
  p. cm.—(Cultures Of The World)
 Includes bibliographical references and index.
 ISBN 0-7614-0281-0 (lib. bdg.)
 1. Cambodia—Juvenile literature. I. Title.
II. Series.
DS554.3.S54 1996
959.6—dc20   95–44453
     CIP
      AC

INTRODUCTION

THE PAST 25 YEARS of Cambodia's history presents a heart-rending story. The country was caught up in the turmoil of the Vietnam War, and then thrown into a nightmare of "auto-genocide," when Cambodians massacred fellow Cambodians—at least three quarters of a million died.

Yet incredibly, the country's culture and identity has survived. Cambodia can justifiably take pride in a rich past preserved in the magnificent temple complex of Angkor. The Cambodian will to survive has triumphed, just as the architectural splendors of Angkor have outlived the savage warfare.

Today Cambodia is in the midst of rebuilding itself—socially, economically, and psychologically. The scars of the past, however, will take decades to heal. This book tells the unique story of a country in the throes of recreating itself. It is a story of terrible suffering, but also a tale of hope.

CONTENTS

Cambodian boys enjoy a game of marbles.

CONTENTS

A young girl displays a piece of cloth for sale.

GEOGRAPHY

WITH A LAND AREA of 69,898 square miles (181,035 square kilometers)—approximately the size of Missouri—Cambodia is one of the smallest nations in Southeast Asia. The Mekong River and the huge lake of Tonle Sap form the country's most important geographical landmarks.

Cambodia is bounded in the north by Thailand and Laos, in the west by Thailand, and in the east by Vietnam. The Gulf of Thailand lies to the south of Cambodia. Most of Cambodia's borders follow the natural courses of rivers. An exception is the eastern border with Vietnam, much of which was artificially created by colonial and other past political rulers. As a result, there are some 50 miles (80 kilometers) of disputed border. The absence of topographic features like rivers and mountains adds to the difficulty of determining the border, causing disputes over whether particular villages belong to Cambodia or Vietnam.

Opposite: **The Mekong River provides food in the form of fish for Cambodians. For centuries, the river has underpinned the fundamental ecology of the country, though a proposed dam threatens to change nature's balance.**

Left: **A bird's-eye view of rice fields near the town of Kampong Chhnang in central Cambodia.**

7

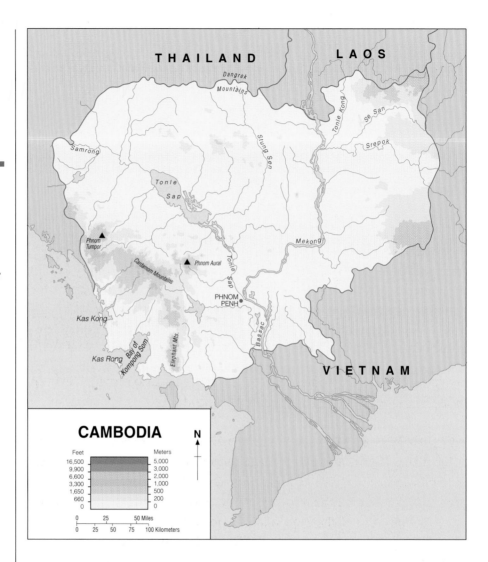

Cambodia's maximum width from east to west is 360 miles (580 kilometers). From north to south, the maximum distance is 279 miles (505 kilometers).

TOPOGRAPHY

About half of Cambodia's total area is covered by forests, but this proportion is decreasing as trees are cut down and exported for foreign exchange. Some 10% of the land is covered by water or swamps. The remaining 40% of the country's territory is arable, although not all of it is actually cultivated.

The Mekong River provides the focus for settled agriculture. Villages are spread out along both banks of the river and its tributaries as well as

near the shores of the Tonle Sap. The various rivers also provide the main means of transport for villagers and their produce.

THE CENTRAL PLAIN Cambodia's most important region is its central plain, where the richness of the land is replenished by the regular flooding of the Mekong River and its tributaries. Over the centuries, people have used the regularity of the flooding as a way of irrigating their fields. The constant watering of the land makes it ideal for the cultivation of rice, which is the country's main source of food. The fertile land also allows for a variety of vegetables to be grown.

In addition, the rivers are a source of fish. With a friendly climate that lacks extremes, Cambodia has favorable conditions for agriculture, which helps explain why the country has, for centuries, managed to escape the periodic famines that have afflicted other countries in this part of the world. The fertility of the alluvial plain also explains why the majority of Cambodians live in this part of the country.

Most of the central plain is gently rolling land; in the south, below the city of Phnom Penh, the plain becomes flatter.

Cambodia produces over 2 million tons (1.82 million metric tons) of rice every year from about 4.5 million acres (1.8 million hectares) of farmland.

Forests near the temple complex of Angkor Wat. The densely forested, underpopulated, and inaccessible mountainous regions of Cambodia have, for the last 15 years, provided a safe haven for the Khmer Rouge forces opposed to the government.

The dense forests and mountains of the eastern highlands extend eastward into the central highlands of neighboring Vietnam as well as northwards into Laos.

MOUNTAINS In the southwest of Cambodia lies a highland region formed by two mountain ranges. One is the granite Cardamom Mountains, which rise to a maximum of 5,000 feet (1,500 meters). The other range is the Elephant Mountains, which form a barrier between the lowlands of the central plain and the coastal region.

Isolated from the activity in the central plain, the southern coastal area remained largely undeveloped until several decades ago. It was not until the 1950s that a port town, Kompong Som, was created. The only connecting road from Kompong Som to the capital, Phnom Penh, was constructed in 1969.

The northern border with Thailand is part of a sandstone escarpment that runs in an east-west direction for over 190 miles (300 kilometers) and ranges in height from 590 to 1,800 feet (180 to 550 meters). In the northeast corner of the country is another mountainous region, reaching as high as 3,000 feet (900 meters), formed by the eastern highlands. This is the most remote part of the country and home to hill tribes that add to the richness of the country's culture.

THE MEKONG RIVER

The Mekong River is the 10th largest river (in volume) in the world. With a length of just over 2,600 miles (4,186 kilometers), it is Southeast Asia's most important river. At some places along its course, it grows to almost three miles (4.8 kilometers) wide.

The Mekong rises in Tibet and runs southward into Laos before entering Cambodia by way of a series of dramatic waterfalls. Once in the Cambodian floodplain, the river becomes navigable for the first time. The navigable portions, open to cargo ships, stretch from north of Phnom Penh to the river's delta in Vietnam. Before entering Cambodia, the Mekong has tremendous turbulence, forming some of the widest rapids in the world over a six-mile (9.7 kilometers) stretch in Laos. In Cambodia, there are also disruptive rapids just northeast of the capital. After flowing through Cambodia for about 315 miles (507 kilometers), the Mekong splits into two branches south of Phnom Penh. The western branch becomes the Bassac River, while the eastern branch retains the name Mekong. Its delta is over 200 miles (320 kilometers) wide and splits into numerous tributaries before flowing into the South China Sea in Vietnam.

It has been estimated that as much as one-fifth of Cambodian land is affected by the annual flooding of the Mekong River during the wet season. This is a valuable process for two reasons. The receding waters leave behind a rich deposit of alluvial soil, which adds to the fertility of the affected land. In addition, a great number of fish are left in the shallow water, providing an important source of food for the people.

Paddling past a floating village on the Tonle Sap. Small boats like this are a common form of transportation on Cambodia's waterways.

TONLE SAP

The literal translation of the name of this natural reservoir is Great Lake. Once it was just another tributary leading to the sea, but the continual silting up of the Mekong delta turned the Tonle Sap into an inland lake. It is connected to the Mekong at Phnom Penh by a 50-mile-long (80-kilometer) channel of water known as the Tonle Sap River.

During the dry season, the Tonle Sap covers about 100 square miles (260 square kilometers) and is never more than five feet (1.5 meters) deep. Between May and October—the wet season—the lower channels of the Mekong become so silted up that the floodwaters build up and cause the Mekong to rise as much as 45 feet (13 meters) above its banks. Some of the surplus water backs up the Tonle Sap River and causes it to reverse its normal flow so that it runs northwestward into the Tonle Sap.

During this wet period, the Tonle Sap's depth increases to as much as 40 to 45 feet (12 to 13 meters), and from its former size of 100 square miles, it can spread to an area of 770 square miles (1,994 square kilometers).

With the return of the dry season, water in the Mekong returns to its lower level and the Tonle Sap river reverses its flow, once again draining its waters back into the Mekong. What is left behind, however, is the richest area of freshwater fishing in the world. Estimates of fish yields are in the region of a million pounds (450,000 kilograms) of fish for every square mile (2.6 square kilometers) of the Tonle Sap.

A CONTROVERSIAL DAM

The theory was first proposed by the United States over 50 years ago: a series of giant dams that would transform Southeast Asia into a giant food basket. At the heart of such a plan is the Mekong River. In 1995, the first practical steps were taken to implement the idea. Cambodia, along with Thailand, Vietnam, and Laos, jointly established the Mekong River Commission.

The plan is to construct a series of six dams that together would generate more than 9,000 megawatts of electricity, flood about 386 square miles (1,000 square kilometers), and be used for irrigation by Cambodia and the other three countries.

Environmentalists have pointed out the catastrophic human and ecological costs of such a plan. Thousands of people would have to leave their homes and farms. The long-term effect could involve irreparable damage to the ecosystem that is sustained by the Mekong River. At present some 50 million people depend on the river—directly and indirectly—for their livelihood, and the possible effects of the six-dam cascade are fraught with uncertainties. Tonle Sap's rich and diverse fish life could also be seriously affected, which would be devastating for millions of Cambodians.

CLIMATE

Two monsoons dominate the annual climatic pattern. Between November and March, there is little rain from a dry, northeastern monsoon. During this period, in December and January, villagers harvest their rice. From May to October, a southwestern monsoon brings heavy rain and strong winds. The rain often falls during the afternoon in a series of intermittent bursts. The southwestern monsoon produces about three-quarters of the country's total annual rainfall.

In the central plain, nearly 72 inches (1.8 meters) of rain falls during the six months of the southwestern monsoon. The east coast of the United States, by comparison, receives about 48 inches (1.2 meters) over 12 months. In between these two periods, during April and May, the weather is a mixture of the two, even though April is also the hottest month of the year.

April is, for the most part, the most uncomfortable month for Cambodians because the air is sticky and the high humidity is only relieved by a few light rain showers. Toward the end of the month, however, the rainy monsoon approaches and the first rains begin to fall. This change in the climate is marked by festivals and New Year celebrations.

During April, the temperature in Phnom Penh averages 80°F (27°C), with daily maximums of 89°F–104°F (32°C–40°C). January, the coldest month, sees an average temperature of 78°F (25.6°C).

FLORA AND FAUNA

The flora of the central lowland region is governed by the importance of agriculture. Rice fields are the most characteristic feature of the landscape, alongside fields of other crops like tobacco and corn. In the north, where mountains predominate, evergreen forests are found. In the southwest there are also forests—tracts of primary forest and teak trees.

Teak is a common tree, although it is not native to Cambodia. It was introduced toward the end of the 17th century. Teak is an important and valuable source of water-resistant timber. Because of its extreme weight, teak will sink in water unless it has been completely dried, so the tree is killed by cutting away its bark and then leaving it for two years before cutting it down. In the future, the teak forests can be expected to provide a valuable export for Cambodia. Pine trees grow at higher elevations in the southwest. Along the 300-mile (530-kilometer) coastline, mangrove forests face the Gulf of Thailand, while along the inland rivers lotuses are common. The lotus of Cambodia, also found in China and India, is considered sacred and is traditionally associated with the Buddha.

Large wild animals that are becoming increasingly rare in most parts of the world continue to roam the Cambodian countryside in comparative safety. Elephants, leopards, tigers, and wild oxen are not uncommon. Before war erupted in the 1970s, affluent game-hunters from around the world regarded Cambodia as prime territory for shooting wild animals.

Cambodia's most unusual animal is the kouprey, a wild forest ox that was only identified in 1939 and is now a symbol of the Worldwide Fund for Nature. The kouprey is almost extinct, with just a few thought to still survive in the most remote parts of the country. Pessimists, however, believe that the hard times caused by the civil war led to the last koupreys being hunted and killed for food.

The country's national symbol is the sugar palm tree. It provides a robust building material and the sap is used to make medicine and wine. The sugar palm tree can grow to a height of about 40 feet (12 meters) and has feathery leaves.

A young rice farmer tills the earth. Plowing with oxen has been done for centuries in Cambodia.

Cambodia has a rich and diverse birdlife, including elegant birds such as pelicans, herons, egrets, and cranes, and colorful ones like tropical parrots and kingfishers. Cormorants, pheasants, and grouse are also common. Fish-eating water fowl are especially common around the Tonle Sap because of the quantities of fish brought in when flooding occurs.

CITIES

Phnom Penh, the capital, is Cambodia's largest city, with an estimated one million people. It is situated at the confluence of the Mekong, Bassac, and Tonle Sap rivers in the central plain. Phnom Penh was founded in 1434 to succeed Angkor Thom as the capital, but was abandoned several times before being reestablished in 1865. Despite being 180 miles (290 kilometers) from the sea, it is a major port, linked to the South China Sea via the Mekong River.

Other urban centers include Batdambang (100,000 people), Kompong Som (66,000), and Kampong Cham (33,000).

Snakes are common in Cambodia. Four species are particularly dangerous—the cobra, the king cobra, Russell's viper, and the banded krait.

15

HISTORY

EVIDENCE OF HABITATION around the Mekong Delta goes back to around 4,000 B.C. It is generally believed that the early inhabitants arrived in two main waves of migration: one from what is now Indonesia and a second moving down from Tibet and China.

India was an early influence in the first millennium when trade routes were established by Indian traders seeking the previously unexplored world of Southeast Asia. The cultural influence of India was profound. Even today, it is evident in crucial areas of Cambodian life, such as religion and language, as well as dance and literature.

FUNAN

A Cambodian legend links the kingdom of Funan with India through an Indian Brahmin priest called Kaundinya. The Brahmin possessed the magic to force anyone he chose into marrying him. He picked Soma, the daughter of the Lord of the Soil (a ruler of the Mekong delta). Their marriage led to the founding of the "Lunar Dynasty" of Funan. As a wedding present, the Lord of the Soil obligingly drank the flooding waters of the Mekong; he thereby enlarged the size of their territory and helped the people to cultivate their land.

The legend is testimony to the importance of Indian influence in the development of the Funan kingdom. It was established around the second or third century A.D. by people from southern China. Its importance resulted from its strategic position in the trading route between India and China. Since merchant ships liked to keep the coast in sight as they turned to the north around the Mekong delta, any coastal settlement was bound to offer itself as a stopping place. Funan's major port was in what is now southern Vietnam, but the kingdom included most of modern Cambodia.

The name Funan is a Chinese transliteration of a Khmer word meaning "hill," suggesting that its seat of power was situated on an elevation—and probably one that could be seen from the sea.

Opposite: **A representation of Suryavarman II, who ruled the Angkor empire from 1113 to 1150. Angkor Wat, the outstanding architectural achievement of his reign, was completed at about the time of his death.**

War scenes from a temple carving. The history of Angkor is punctuated by wars with its neighbors, Thailand and Vietnam.

THE ANGKORIAN ERA

In the sixth century, the Funan kingdom splintered, and a period of instability followed. In the eighth century, present-day Cambodia was taken over by Java (now part of Indonesia).

The first ruler to be associated with the dynasty based around Angkor was Jayavarman II. He was of Javanese origin, but his importance is due to his assertion of independence from Java. Equally significant was his declaration of god-given powers. He proclaimed himself more than a king—he was a god-king, allied to the king of the Hindu gods, Shiva. It was during the reign of his nephew, Indravarman (who ruled between 877 and 889), that large-scale irrigation of the Mekong River began.

As the system of irrigation was developed and extended, a more settled agricultural society was created. The resulting stability led to an increase both in population and in the power of the ruling dynasty. Under the rule of Yasovarman, the capital was moved to the area around Angkor. This was the first step in what would become an astonishing flowering of artistic confidence, expressed in architecture and sculpture, that continues to fascinate the world.

Apart from a brief period in the 10th century, Angkor remained the political and cultural heart of Cambodia until the middle of the 15th century. The interruption was caused by an invasion from Vietnam, which resulted in the sacking of Angkor. When Khmer rule was restored by Jayavarman VII (1181–1201), there was a need to rebuild Angkor. What followed was an ambitious and impressive program of reconstruction, and the major site of Angkor Thom came into being.

DECLINE AND FALL OF ANGKOR

Historians offer differing explanations for the demise of Angkor. But all agree that the growing hostility of neighboring Thailand was a prime factor. Thai rulers made constant attempts to destabilize their Angkorian rivals in an attempt to extend their own territory. Each attempted invasion from Thailand disrupted the elaborate irrigation system on which Angkorian society depended. The need to militarize the country also slowed down—and eventually stopped—the upkeep of the temples and the building of new ones. The temples existed to sanctify the rule of the god-kings. When they fell into a state of disrepair, it revealed the weakening hold of the rulers over their people.

By the middle of the 15th century, Angkor had fallen to Thailand. The rulers deserted their capital and retreated to an area around Phnom Penh. For the next century and a half, an ongoing war was fought between the Thais and Khmers. The Thais were pushed back out of the country, but in 1594 they returned in force and Angkor was again occupied.

Until the arrival of the French, Cambodia was ruled by various kings. The kings were continually fighting off challenges to their power from within their own royal families. Alliances were made with either Thailand or Vietnam to gain military support and in return, Thais and Vietnamese were allowed to settle in the respective border regions. During this period, the Vietnamese began to populate what is now the southern region of Vietnam, then a part of Cambodia.

An enigmatic Buddha head at the Bayon, near Siem Reap.

19

ARRIVAL OF THE FRENCH

By the 1860s, Cambodia was in imminent danger of being completely absorbed by either Thai or Vietnamese rule. Both countries were able to invade Cambodia at will; only their own rivalry kept Cambodia intact. As a result, in 1863, the French had little difficulty persuading King Norodom to sign a treaty placing the kingdom under French protection.

Cambodia was incorporated into a Union of Indochina, governed by a resident-general based in Hanoi. French administrators were introduced. Slavery was abolished and modern schools were built. The Khmer elite received French education and were introduced to French culture. To maintain order and dampen any threat of nationalist sentiment, the French continued to support the monarchy.

In the early 1940s, Japan seized *de facto* control of Cambodia. Cambodia was now part of Japan's "Greater East Asia Co-prosperity Sphere." The provinces of Batdambang and Siem Reap were ceded to Thailand, while the French were allowed to retain nominal control in the rest of the country. After Japan's surrender, ending World War II, the two northwestern provinces were returned by Thailand, and Cambodia was recognized as an autonomous kingdom within the French Union.

By then, a growing sense of Cambodian nationalism was brewing. In 1953, Prince Norodom Sihanouk, who had been crowned king in 1941, proclaimed his country independent of France. He began a crusade to gather international support, and before the end of 1954, the French had to accept that Cambodia was no longer one of their colonies.

INDEPENDENCE

The first two decades of independence were difficult times for Cambodia. Sihanouk had to contend with domestic threats to his rule, and in 1955 he

Between 1603 and 1848, the date of the last Cambodian ruler to assume the throne free from French political control, 22 monarchs occupied the throne. Several of these rulers had more than one reign, as they gave up their position either through choice or under duress, only to return when their successors proved incapable or were themselves deposed.

abdicated the throne in order to establish his own political party. A parliament had been created after independence so the monarchy could no longer exercise absolute rule. Sihanouk's party easily won control of parliament.

In the 1960s, Cambodia's neighbor, Vietnam, became increasingly embroiled in a civil war that also involved the United States. At first Sihanouk proclaimed his country's neutrality, but neutrality became increasingly more difficult. By 1965, Sihanouk felt that the United States was conspiring against him because of his refusal to support South Vietnam in its war against North Vietnam. Cambodia turned instead to North Vietnam and allowed the Viet Cong to use its territory as a base in its war against the Americans.

In 1969 the United States began a secret bombing of suspected Viet Cong bases in Cambodia. The bombing continued for four years and increased in scope until vast areas in the east of the country were being systematically carpet-bombed by U.S. B-52s. In March 1970, Sihanouk was deposed by Lon Nol, one of his generals, with U.S. support, and the country was invaded by U.S. and South Vietnamese troops.

An Independence Day parade in 1955. Prince Sihanouk abdicated in March 1955 to found a mass movement, the Popular Socialist Community. The movement won all the seats in elections to the National Assembly in 1955, 1958, 1962, and 1966.

Mass graves from the Pol Pot era. After coming to power in 1975, Khmer Rouge leader Pol Pot began a program of genocide in which religious groups, ethnic minorities, and other Cambodians perceived to be enemies of the Khmer Rouge were systematically executed.

KHMER ROUGE RULE

Cambodia's new ruler, Lon Nol, presided over an increasingly corrupt administration. Guerilla armies withdrew from the towns and began gaining influence over the countryside. Hundreds of thousands of people died in the fighting that engulfed the country. Even military and financial support from the United States could not stem the tide of civil war. In April 1975, the capital, Phnom Penh, flooded by well over a million refugees, fell to the Khmer Rouge, who became the new rulers of Cambodia.

The Khmer Rouge leadership had concluded that Cambodia's problems were the result of its colonial history. Its solution was that the country should return to a primitive, self-sufficient agricultural state. Returning to the past—to "Year Zero"—meant abolishing money, schools, 20th-century technology, and newspapers. The idea of the family and of life in a town or city was regarded as antirevolutionary. This meant emptying cities of their entire population (Phnom Penh became a ghost town), breaking up families, and imposing a collective agriculture. All this was accomplished under a rule of extreme harshness that resulted in the death of at least 750,000 civilians. People died from lack of food or from disease. Doctors, like teachers and other middle class professionals, were executed for being antirevolutionary, and hospitals were closed down. Many others died from overwork.

VIETNAMESE INVASION

At the end of 1978, the Vietnamese army poured across the border and swiftly brought to an end the rule of Pol

Phnom Penh fell to Vietnamese forces on January 7, 1979. Three days later, the People's Republic of Kampuchea was proclaimed under the leadership of Heng Samrin.

Pot and the Khmer Rouge. Vietnam had invaded Cambodia to protect its western territory from hostile raids by the Khmer Rouge. Although Vietnam had liberated Cambodia from tyranny, the rest of the world was reluctant to recognize the puppet government installed in Phnom Penh.

American hostility to Vietnam played a large part in ensuring that Pol Pot's Democratic Kampuchea kept its seat at the United Nations. Cambodians suffered the aftermath of a disrupted rice harvest brought about by the Vietnamese invasion, and many died. Only an international famine relief program rescued the country from a devastating famine.

By 1985, the Vietnamese had forced the Khmer Rouge into Thailand. From there, Pol Pot's army continued to plague the country by mounting guerilla attacks and planting thousands of land mines that continue to take an annual toll of Cambodian lives.

Vietnam's intervention in Cambodia lasted for nearly 11 years. It ended when Mikhail Gorbachev's new Soviet Union began to press for withdrawal. By the end of 1989, the last Vietnamese troops had left Cambodia.

The UNTAC Headquarters in Phnom Penh. Its mandate was terminated in September 1993, after the promulgation of the new Cambodian Constitution.

PEACE AT LAST?

An internationally sponsored peace agreement was signed in Paris in 1991. Early the next year, the United Nations Transitional Authority in Cambodia (UNTAC) arrived to pave the way for democratic elections. The signatories to the peace plan included representatives from most of the political groups that had held or sought power in Cambodia over the previous two decades. A new coalition government emerged, dedicated to building a new future. The Khmer Rouge signed the peace treaty, but then failed to honor its terms. It decided to boycott the elections. Today, from their stronghold in the northwest of the country, the Khmer Rouge continues to pose a threat to Cambodia's peace.

WHAT'S IN A NAME?

Kampuchea is the Cambodian word for Cambodia. The word comes from *kambu-ja* ("kam-BOO-jah"), meaning "born of Kambu" (a figure from Indian mythology). In the last 50 years, however, the country has changed its name six times:

- The Kingdom of Cambodia—1953–1970
- The Khmer Republic—1970–1975
- Democratic Kampuchea—1975–1979
- The People's Republic of Kampuchea—1979–1989
- The State of Cambodia—1989–1993
- The Kingdom of Cambodia—1993–present

The changes reflect the years in which important political changes took place. Each new political order wanted to separate itself from the previous political system. Changing the name of the country was a dramatic—and drastic—means. The Khmer Rouge insisted that the rest of the world recognize the country's name as Kampuchea. Vietnam retained the name after taking control in 1979. In 1989, when the country regained control of its own affairs, the name Cambodia was readopted to symbolize the discrediting of the Khmer Rouge. The government of the time felt that a new country was being created and the linguistic change was needed to reflect this.

GOVERNMENT

IN 1993, THE UNITED NATIONS mounted what was then the biggest (22,000 troops) and most expensive (US$2 billion) peace operation in its history. The aim was to manage a general election in Cambodia, a country that had been torn apart and almost destroyed by more than 20 years of civil war.

The United Nations managed to register 4.8 million voters, established over 1,400 polling stations, and brought back 360,000 refugees, who had been living in camps in Thailand. Some 50,000 Cambodians were trained by the United Nations to staff the elections. Another 1,400 officials were recruited from other countries for two weeks to lend authority to the process. Candidates from 20 parties registered for election. The four warring factions that signed the Paris Peace Agreement in 1991 formed the main political parties.

Opposite: **The Monument of Independence in Phnom Penh. Cambodia's independence was formally announced on November 9, 1953.**

Left: **Poll workers prepare for the 1993 elections. Many Cambodians journeyed long distances by foot, bicycle, and bullock cart across some of the most heavily mined countryside in the world to cast their vote.**

The typical voter in the 1993 elections was a woman, the head of a household, who had lost her husband in one of the country's wars.

The Khmer Rouge became the Party of Democratic Kampuchea (PDK). The Vietnamese-backed government that ran Cambodia following Vietnam's invasion in 1978 became the Cambodian People's Party (CPP). A royalist group headed by Prince Norodom Sihanouk's son, Norodom Ranariddh, reverted to its old name, the National United Front for an Independent, Neutral, Peaceful, and Cooperative Cambodia (FUNCINPEC), while a non-Communist group headed by Son Sann split into the Buddhist Liberal Democratic Party (BLDP) and the Liberal Democratic Party (LDP).

The PDK, or Khmer Rouge, having gained some legitimacy by signing the Paris Peace Agreement, then denounced the elections and threatened to disrupt them. Pessimists predicted that the elections would be rendered meaningless by guerilla tactics from dissident groups. During the election in May 1993, some Cambodians were killed. Nevertheless, by the time polling closed, a very large percentage of the electorate (some 90%) had turned out to exercise their right to vote.

THE ELECTION RESULTS

The elections were considered a success by international observers. As expected, no one party emerged a clear victor. The three parties that won the most seats in the 120-member National Assembly were FUNCINPEC (58 seats), the CPP (51 seats), and the BLDP (10 seats). These parties, though representing different policies and ideologies, were forced into an alliance in order to form a government. Votes accorded to the CPP recognized that, despite being installed by the Vietnamese military, the party saved the country from Pol Pot. The votes given to FUNCINPEC reflected the strong anti-Vietnam and anti-Communist sentiment in the country. In October 1993 Prince Ranariddh of FUNCINPEC was installed as first prime minister, with Hun Sen of the CPP as second prime minister.

PRINCE NORODOM SIHANOUK

As a young god-king, Sihanouk (shown above, waving to the crowd) surprised the French by championing the nationalist cause and campaigning for their withdrawal. After independence his royalty became a hindrance because the constitution curtailed the political powers of the monarch. He then abdicated the throne to become a full-time politician.

At different times he has been associated with widespread corruption and abuse of human rights, and observers accuse him of egotism and vanity. After fleeing to China after the Vietnamese invasion, he was quite prepared to join forces with the Khmer Rouge in a coalition aimed at regaining political control of the country. At the same time, Sihanouk is the nearest Cambodia has to a revered national leader. Because of the outrages under Pol Pot, there is a tendency to look back to Sihanouk's Cambodia of the 1960s as a golden age of tranquillity and progress. His political opponents received harsh treatment, but compared to what came later under the Khmer Rouge, his period of rule seems a benign one to many observers.

In the negotiations of the early 1990s, he emerged once again as a figure who could represent the notion of Cambodia as a united country. After an absence of 38 years, he was returned to the throne in 1993 as the king of Cambodia. Now that he is over 70 years old and seriously ill, Cambodia's challenge is to find new figures to represent a government for the future.

Prince Norodom Sihanouk was born on October 31, 1922. He succeeded his grandfather as king in April 1941. In March 1955, he abdicated in favor of his father in order to enter politics. He regained his throne in September 1993 after a parliamentary monarchy was re-established by Cambodia's 1993 Constitution.

Khmer Rouge guerillas. Most Cambodians have lost at least one relative to the Khmer Rouge. Fear of a return to the 1975–78 years is perhaps the country's best hope for stability in the future.

THE KHMER ROUGE FACTOR

Within months of forming a government, Ranariddh ordered the country's army to mount a series of offensives against the Khmer Rouge guerillas. Thousands of guerillas turned in their arms and defected to the government.

Whether the Khmer Rouge leadership can be persuaded to abandon armed struggle and strike a peace with the new government remains unanswered. Continued economic development and the creation of more jobs will give dispossessed groups less incentive to turn to violence.

The next elections may well see the PDK participating as a legal party. Present estimates put the number of active Khmer Rouge guerillas at between 5,000 and 7,500.

CHALLENGES FOR THE NEW GOVERNMENT

When the United Nations left Cambodia after the elections, an immediate problem emerged over who would maintain law and order. It will be some time before the new unified Cambodian army is able to function effectively. Creating an army and police force free of corruption is another challenge facing the government.

Even more fundamental is the task of creating a government. Under the Khmer Rouge regime there was a systematic destruction of intellectuals and professionals. Those who managed to escape death fled the country. The country faces a dire shortage of educated and middle-class professionals

THE MYSTERIOUS POL POT

His real name is Saloth Sar and he was born into a peasant family in 1928. Not academically outstanding at school, he nevertheless won a scholarship to study in Paris. It was there that he further developed his Communist ideas, which had first taken shape while he was in school in Phnom Penh. His interest in politics eventually lost him his scholarship, and he returned to Cambodia in its early years of independence. In 1963, he fled into the countryside, where he rose through the ranks of the Communist Party of Kampuchea to become its secretary-general. He trained in guerilla tactics, and by the time Khmer Rouge forces took over the capital in 1975, he was the undisputed leader.

For the vast majority of Cambodians, so many of whom suffered terribly under his regime, Pol Pot has remained a shadowy figure. He was never the subject of a personality cult and his name meant nothing to the millions of people who endured the return to "Year Zero." Pol Pot is a recluse. When his troops took the capital in 1975, he did not appear in any of the victory parades that followed. He entered the city quietly, after it had been emptied of people. Very few foreigners have ever seen him and only a handful have ever spoken to him.

Pol Pot is still alive and, as far as is known, still in charge of the Khmer Rouge forces that inhabit an increasingly smaller border area between Thailand and Cambodia. His influence is decreasing, but the thousands of land mines laid by his troops continue to maim civilians. Since the 1980s, a National Hate Day has been held every May 20, providing an opportunity for Cambodians to renounce everything he stands for. Gatherings of civilians take place at village cemeteries and sites associated with former atrocities, and the crimes of the past are remembered in an attempt to come to terms with them. The present government is winning the war against the remnants of Pol Pot's guerilla army. What has happened to Pol Pot himself, however, remains a mystery.

able to put together and run a government.

There is also the problem of the absence of a legal framework or an independent judiciary. A 20-year interruption in normal civil life presents enormous problems for any government. Aspects of life that most countries take for granted, like going to court, for example, when there is a dispute over the legality of an act or business contract, have to be brought into existence in a country that has been forced to manage without them.

Despite the recent history of Cambodia, the country has managed to create a remarkably open society in many respects. Debates in the National Assembly are televised live, and there are often open discussions of the problems facing the country.

Cambodia has fewer than 20 lawyers at present. Phnom Penh University is expected to graduate its first batch of lawyers, about 100, in 1997.

Cambodia's national anthem is Jham Kraham Cral (Bright Red Blood Was Spilt).

THE CONSTITUTION

Cambodia's present constitution was passed in September 1993. Cambodia is a constitutional monarchy. The main provisions of the constitution are:

The King The king is the head of state and supreme commander of the Khmer Royal Armed Forces. The king appoints the prime minister and the cabinet, and holds office for life.

In the event of the king's death, the Throne Council (composed of the chairman of the National Assembly, the prime minister, the supreme patriarchs of Cambodia's two main Buddhist groups, and the first and second vice-chairpersons of the National Assembly) must select a new king from among descendants of three royal lines within seven days.

National Assembly Legislative power lies with the National Assembly, which has at least 120 members. Members are elected to a term of five years by universal adult suffrage. Only Cambodian citizens by birth who are over the age of 25 can stand for election to the National Assembly.

Cabinet The cabinet is led by a prime minister and assisted by deputy prime ministers. Other members of the cabinet are state ministers, ministers, and state secretaries. The prime minister appoints the members of the cabinet, who must be representatives in the National Assembly or members of parties represented in the National Assembly.

The Constitution Council The Constitution Council interprets the constitution and laws passed by the National Assembly. The Council consists of nine members with a nine-year mandate. One-third of the

members are appointed by the king, three elected by the National Assembly, and three appointed by the Supreme Council of the Magistracy.

The National Assembly building in Phnom Penh is the seat of Cambodia's highest legislative body.

Under the present power-sharing scheme, the Cambodian government has two prime ministers. The first prime minister is Prince Norodom Ranariddh of the FUNCINPEC. Hun Sen of the CPP is the second prime minister. The rest of the ministerial positions in the cabinet are shared by the FUNCINPEC, the CPP, and the BLDP. Cambodia's next general election is due in 1998.

ECONOMY

THE ECONOMIC PROBLEMS facing Cambodia in the 1990s are enormous. Over the decades of civil war, few businesses paid taxes. At one stage in the early 1990s, the inflation rate was 90% a month, and the country's unit of currency—the riel—was almost worthless.

After the election of 1993, the government that emerged had to rebuild a viable economy from scratch. The new administration took immediate steps to bolster the country's weak economy: business taxes were collected and all commercial enterprises were required to maintain a record of their financial transactions. The currency has now been stabilized and inflation has been brought under control.

To help reduce corruption within its own ranks, the government awarded civil servants a 20% pay raise. Civil servants now take home an

The average Cambodian worker earns US$170 a year.

Opposite: **Rice farmers at work. The year 1994 was bad for rice harvests as floods, followed by insufficient rain, destroyed as much as a third of Cambodia's rice crop.**

Left: **Watering vegetables at a Khmer Rouge camp. Cambodia produced some 525,000 tons (478,000 metric tons) of vegetables and melons in 1992.**

average of US$30 a month, a good salary by Cambodian standards. Custom officials were given power to double the import duty for anyone caught smuggling and to keep half the amount as a reward.

When the Khmer Rouge set out to return the country to "Year Zero," they envisioned a pre-industrial-age society in which money had no place. This policy devastated the Cambodian economy, which had already been weakened by years of civil war.

After the Vietnamese overthrew the Khmer Rouge, Western nations imposed a trade-and-aid embargo, hampering Vietnamese attempts to rebuild a working economy. The 1990s have seen foreign aid reach Cambodia, and many foreign companies are now keen to invest in the country.

The remaining Khmer Rouge guerillas remain a thorn in Cambodia's economy. One out of every 50 Cambodians is a soldier, and half the national budget is devoted to the armed forces. While this helps provide employment, it is a heavy burden on the country's resources.

The growth of the economy is also seriously handicapped by a lack of skilled labor, the result of disrupted education during the years of civil war. The Vietnamese once provided much-needed skills, but many left the country in the early 1990s.

AGRICULTURE

The overwhelming majority of Cambodians, well over 80%, seek a living from agriculture. However, partly due to the lack of fertilizer, which most farmers cannot afford to purchase, rice yields are among the lowest in the world.

One strain of rice—known as floating rice—is unique to Cambodia. The rice alters its rate of growth to allow for the rise of the floodwaters. The grain heads remain above the water at all times, hence the term floating rice.

The country's food supply has been severely damaged by over two decades of militarization. In the late 1960s, the country was able to export half a million tons (455,000 metric tons) of rice every year. Today Cambodia has difficulty feeding its own population. The United Nations continues to make up the deficit in the annual rice crop, providing 150,000 tons (136,500 metric tons) of rice in 1995.

The next most important crop is corn, followed by cash crops. The

Above: **Farm workers threshing rice. Agriculture accounted for about 45% of Cambodia's Gross Domestic Product in 1992.**

Opposite: **Soldiering is one of the country's most common occupations today. However, if government plans to reduce its armed forces are carried out, more jobs will have to be created in other sectors of the economy.**

Fishing is a mainstay of the Cambodian economy. In 1991, 122,000 tons (111,000 metric tons) of fish were caught.

principal cash crop is rubber. In 1991, Cambodia had about 127,000 acres (52,000 hectares) of rubber plantations, down from almost 170,000 acres (70,000 hectares) in the late 1960s. The largest and oldest plantation is found in the province of Kampong Cham. Some US$12.6 million of rubber latex was exported in 1992. Other cash crops include cotton, tobacco, pepper, and sugar palms.

Apart from rice, fishing is the most important source of food for most Cambodians. The majority of villages exist close to a waterway or have large ponds to provide fish. Around 50% of all fish caught and consumed is taken from the Tonle Sap lake. The fishing season lasts from October to February.

MINERALS

There are no known significant deposits of minerals in Cambodia. Limited deposits of iron ore, limestone, kaolin, tin, bauxite, and silver have been found, but are not exploited commercially.

Since 1991, some small-scale gold mining has taken place in the province of Kampong Cham. Deposits of phosphates are located in the southern province of Kampot and are processed in plants located in Batdambang and Kampot for use as fertilizers. About 5,000 tons (4,550 metric tons) have been produced every year since 1988.

There is a rich potential for oil and natural gas in Cambodia. Foreign companies have already begun competing to drill both onshore and offshore. Another potential industry is precious gems, such as rubies and sapphires. Mined in the region of Batdambang, the trade is still largely in the hands of the Khmer Rouge, which leases out concessions. In 1991, the Khmer Rouge earned some US$2–5 million a month from such mining and related activities.

In September 1994, oil and natural gas was discovered by a British oil company about 124 miles (200 kilometers) southwest of Kompong Som.

PANNING EARTH

Trucks operate 24 hours a day removing earth from Cambodian soil and transporting it across the border to Thailand. The earth is deposited in Thailand and then panned for valuable gemstones. The United Nations has described the result as a "lunar landscape."

Trade in gemstones is largely in the hands of illegal groups; little of the profits made find their way into the mainstream economy of the country. Khmer Rouge units, if not engaging directly in the smuggling of gems out of the country, benefit from the levies they impose on the trade.

Some legal panning also takes place within the country, but the residue soil is washed away into the Tonle Sap River, where it adds to the siltation problem. Fish have been reported to be dying in the river and fisherfolk have to avoid the most muddied areas of the lake.

A logging truck near Siem Reap. Between 1969 and 1993, the forest cover in Cambodia was reduced from 73% of the country's land area to 49%.

FORESTRY

Cambodia's forests are one of the country's most valuable resources. Between 1969 and 1993, some 10.5 million acres (4.3 million hectares) of forests were exploited—representing nearly a quarter of Cambodia's land area. Several provinces have been denuded, and the people suffer from shortages of firewood. Increasing domestic and international concerns about excessive logging eventually led to a ban on the export of unprocessed timber in May 1995. Logging camps in remote areas are believed to be still operating, trucking their timber across border checkpoints controlled by Khmer Rouge guerillas to Thailand.

There is already evidence that the widespread deforestation is damaging the country's natural irrigation system. The increasingly severe problems of drought and flash flooding in recent years, disrupting rice cultivation and fish production, are widely believed to be linked to the loss of forest cover.

TOURISM

In the 1960s, well over 60,000 people visited Cambodia every year. At the time, this was an enviable figure for a Southeast Asian country. The outbreak of civil war reduced this source of income to a trickle.

Between 1988 and 1991, for example, only some 3,000 tourists visited Cambodia each year. Since the signing of the Paris Peace Agreement in 1991, tourists have begun returning in numbers, attracted by the historical sites at Angkor.

In 1993, there were some 120,000 visitors, and ambitious plans are afoot to revive tourism and multiply the number of foreign visitors. But the specter of the Khmer Rouge, continuing banditry in the countryside, and huge numbers of land mines threaten to undermine these efforts.

The Cambodiana is Phnom Penh's largest hotel. Hotel services have markedly improved since 1991 with the growing influx of foreign investors into the industry.

The train station in Phnom Penh is the hub of Cambodia's rail system. Overcrowding is often a problem.

TRANSPORTATION

In 1992, Cambodia had about 9,200 miles (14,800 kilometers) of roads, of which only about 1,600 miles (2,600 kilometers) were asphalted. Many stretches of road were in a state of disrepair. Nevertheless, the situation is improving as rehabilitation projects progress.

There are rail links from Phnom Penh to Batdambang and Kompong Som, but railway tracks in many other parts of the country are in bad repair.

Inland water transportation is vital in Cambodia; some 1,180 miles (1,900 kilometers) of the Mekong-Tonle Sap and Bassac rivers are navigable. The port at Phnom Penh can receive small ocean-going vessels via ports in Vietnam.

Air transportation is rapidly growing. By 1993, domestic air services to Kampong Cham, Siem Reap (site of Angkor Wat), and Stoeng Treng had been restored. The national carrier, Royal Air Cambodge, is also being reestablished.

INDUSTRY

Cambodia has only light industrial factories. In towns, there are factories producing household goods, textiles, soft drinks, alcohol, nails, jute sacks, tires, farm tools, pharmaceutical products, cigarettes, and other light consumer goods.

Most plants operate at low capacity because of periodic shortages of electricity, raw materials, and spare parts. Poor management is also a contributing factor to the low productivity.

In rural areas, many of the estimated 1,500 rice mills that had been constructed before 1970 are back in operation after receiving aid-donated equipment.

Industry accounted for some 16% of the country's Gross Domestic Product in 1992.

Repairing bicycle tires in Phnom Penh. Increasingly, such street-side businesses are springing up in the city as Phnom Penh develops.

FOREIGN TRADE AND INVESTMENT

Cambodia's principal exports include rubber, soybeans, sesame, tobacco, fisheries products, and, until recently, timber. In 1992, total exports amounted to US$265 million. Imports, which include motor vehicles, cigarettes, and petroleum products, totaled US$351 million in 1992.

Singapore is Cambodia's largest trading partner, with two-way trade amounting to over US$400 million in 1994. With some US$260 million invested in the country, Singapore is also Cambodia's second largest foreign investor behind Malaysia (with about US$1.5 billion invested).

43

CAMBODIANS

THE LAST CENSUS, taken in 1962, revealed a population of 5.7 million. The latest 1993 estimates place the population at around 9.3 million. Some 10% of Cambodians live in the capital city of Phnom Penh.

The years of warfare and the severe disruption to normal life slowed down population growth, but the last few years have seen a dramatic increase in the birth rate—an indication of the country's newfound confidence. The present rate of population growth—over 3% a year—is one of the highest in the world.

The years of Khmer Rouge rule distorted the composition of the Cambodian population. Today, about half of the population is under 15. There are nearly 250,000 orphaned children, and the population is disproportionately female, with only 90.5 men for every 100 women.

The average national population density is under 139 people per square mile (54 people per square kilometer). Even in the central lowlands, where living conditions are better, the population density is around 260 per square mile (100 per square kilometer). By comparison, the most prosperous parts of neighboring Vietnam have a density some 10 times greater.

In 1960, the urban population made up 11% of the total population. Today, it is about 15%, even though industrial activity has yet to be restored to prewar levels. Like many less developed countries around the world, rural migration to towns continues to be a significant problem in Cambodia.

KHMERS

Some 90% of Cambodians classify themselves as Khmer. Although their origins are unknown, Khmers probably represent a mixture of Mongol and Melanesian elements. Other accounts suggest that they first came from what is now Malaysia and Indonesia.

On the whole, Khmers are taller and slightly darker than their neighbors, the Thais and the Vietnamese. Khmers have curly hair—it is usually cut short—which also differentiates them from their neighbors. Khmers have intermarried with the other ethnic groups within the country, so there is some variation in physical characteristics.

Until recently, the vast majority of Khmers were content to live in the countryside. The running of small businesses was left to the Chinese and Vietnamese. The Khmer people preferred to work their own farms, where they owned the land themselves, and were more or less self-sufficient. Most Khmers still work as farmers, but since 1991, increasing numbers have migrated to Phnom Penh and other urban areas. Moreover, because many Chinese and Vietnamese have left Cambodia, Khmers are moving into commercial activities that were once considered alien to them.

Khmers of both sexes wear a loose-fitting wrap-around garment called a *sampot* ("SAM-pot"). Made of cotton or silk, it is a cross between trousers

and a dress. A loose jacket or blouse that comes down to about the waist is worn over the *sampot*. A straw hat, usually pointed, is often worn. A large scarf, known as a *kramar* ("cray-MAR"), is worn around the neck to protect the skin from the sun.

For everyday work, the traditional form of dress is the *sarong* ("sah-RONG"), a length of cloth that is wrapped around the waist. It is worn by both men and women. Shorts are also common among men who work in the countryside. Footware often consists of loose rubber sandals, but it is not unusual to see men and women walking barefoot.

Opposite and above: **With nine out of every 10 Cambodians belonging to the Khmer ethnic group, Cambodia has the most homogeneous population in Southeast Asia.**

A pair of Vietnamese girls. The Vietnamese favor a robe-like outer garment with a split at the sides, with pajama-style trousers to match. For formal occasions, the women's robe reaches above the ankles. For men, it is cut short around the knees. The typical two-piece black cotton suit is a distinguishing feature of Vietnamese dress and differentiates them from the Khmer.

VIETNAMESE

The number of Vietnamese living in Cambodia has fluctuated in recent years. Before 1970, there were at least 250,000 ethnic Vietnamese living in Cambodia. A chief means of livelihood was fishing in the Tonle Sap region and running small shops in the capital and other population centers.

The present estimate is still somewhere in the region of 250,000, although the real figure may be much higher. Under French colonial rule, the Vietnamese were encouraged to settle in the country. Many came, attracted by the opportunies. Under Pol Pot, they were forced to flee or, in many cases, forcibly expelled. They had little choice but to settle in Vietnam—a country that most of them knew little about. After Vietnam invaded Cambodia in late 1978, they began to return.

Some ethnic rivalry exists between the Vietnamese and the Khmer. In part, this springs from the different lifestyles and aspirations of the two groups. The Vietnamese are more work-oriented, partly because Vietnam is a far more densely populated country. This has forced the Vietnamese to struggle for farmland and to work hard to make a living.

By comparison, Cambodia has historically been a less densely populated country and one where the inhabitants have been able to earn a living more easily.

CHINESE

Chinese immigrants first arrived in Cambodia in the third century B.C. The largest influx occurred in the second half of the 19th century and during the 20th century, mostly from southeastern China. By 1968, there were some 250,000 Chinese in Cambodia.

Their economic importance to the country was far greater than their numerical presence might suggest. In many respects, especially in the capital and other towns, they controlled the economic life of the country. Under Pol Pot, however, they were singled out as ideological enemies and persecuted.

Traditionally, the Chinese have made their living as merchants and traders. This made them particularly vulnerable during the Pol Pot years, when any form of business was outlawed.

When the Vietnamese invaded Cambodia in 1978, many Chinese who had managed to survive chose to emigrate. A steady exodus continued in the years that followed. Only since 1991 has this emigration slowed down.

A Chinese language class for children. In the return to "Year Zero," people who depended on buying and selling for their livelihood had no place in society. Consequently, the Chinese suffered terribly, and thousands were executed during the Pol Pot years.

CHAMS

The Chams are the remnants of a great Champa civilization that was one of the earliest Hindu-influenced states of Southeast Asia. For over 1,000 years, the kingdom of Champa flourished, despite wars with the Chinese and Khmers, until it was finally conquered by the Vietnamese in the 15th century.

Many of the dispossessed people settled in Cambodia, where they managed to avoid servitude under the Vietnamese. There, the Chams were converted to Islam and assimilated by Malay traders. Under Pol Pot, they were persecuted for not sharing the ideology of the Khmer Rouge.

Physically, Chams are darker than Khmers, and have sharper features and more body hair. The dress of the Chams is similar to the Malay dress worn in Malaysia and Indonesia. Like the Khmers, men wear *sarongs*, while women are often seen in long-sleeved jackets.

Current estimates put the number of Chams in Cambodia at about 240,000. Most live in a couple of hundred villages clustered along the Mekong River to the east and north of the capital. By tradition, Cham men are cattle dealers, fishermen, and boat builders. Cham women are renowned as silk and mat weavers.

HILL TRIBES

A variety of ethnic groups are designated under the term hill tribes because they share the same physical environment—the highland plateaus and valleys, which are heavily forested and surrounded by mountains. These groups include the Saoch in the Elephant Mountains, the Pear in the Cardamom Mountains, and along the border with Laos in the northeast, the Krung, Jarai, and Tampuan. In the far northwest of the country lives the Kuy tribe.

The various hill tribes have never integrated with mainstream Cambodian life; this has helped them to preserve their own culture and lifestyle. Because of their geographical isolation, they managed to avoid becoming victims of Pol Pot's genocidal campaigns against ethnic minorities.

People of the hill tribes have a distinctive appearance because of the importance attached to personal decoration. Their ears are pierced, and the lobes are often elongated to support heavy rings. Heavier bangles are worn around the ankles and wrists. Tattoos are not as common as they once were but are still to be found.

"If I want 10, I'll shoot 10 [animals], and if I want 20, I'll shoot 20."

—Traditional boast of a hill tribe hunter

Opposite: **A Cham Muslim. Being Muslims, the Cham were singled out for persecution under Pol Pot.**

THE POLITICS OF COLOR

Under Pol Pot, Cambodians were forbidden to wear colored clothes. Such items were associated with the cities, which had been forcibly evacuated and condemned as decadent. The Khmer Rouge themselves always dressed in black. Cambodians from the towns, who were forced into the countryside, had to dye their clothes black by dipping their garments into a liquid made from boiling the leaves of trees, and then rolling them in mud.

Today, with the reinstatement of Buddhism as the national religion, the saffron robes of monks are once again to be seen. Their bright color signals the return of a more open society.

LIFESTYLE

THERE IS A TRADITIONAL CAMBODIAN ATTITUDE to life that is the result of centuries of Buddhist teaching. The present life is viewed as only one stage in a broader movement of life where one is repeatedly reborn. Consequently, there is a tendency to accept one's present situation in life as something preordained. The idea that one ought to work hard in order to make more money and improve the quality of life is at odds with traditional Cambodian beliefs. Working to provide sufficient food for oneself and one's family is seen in Buddhist terms as an end in itself. Being ambitious is not necessarily regarded as virtuous.

Similarly, there is a belief system that discourages feelings of envy towards those who obviously have more money or possessions. It has been observed that such a philosophy allows the poor to remain poor, while allowing a more privileged minority to escape responsibility for society at large. Part of the extreme ideology of the Khmer Rouge was a total rejection of this philosophical acceptance of inequality. Pol Pot stood for egalitarianism in a very literal way; his ideas were a radical rejection of a traditional lifestyle that had governed the country for centuries.

Above: **Young people are brought up to accept and respect others. This includes accepting relative differences in social class.**

Opposite: **For many river-dwelling Cambodians, a boat is their most precious material possession.**

The traditional attitude to life was not destroyed by Pol Pot's regime. It is still in evidence today and helps to explain the great importance that is still attached to personal relationships. Showing respect for one's family relations, especially those who are older, is still an integral part of a young person's upbringing. In theory at least, it is extended to society at large.

A war-damaged street in Phnom Penh. The city once had a population of some 1.8 million (in 1972). Virtually the entire population was evacuated in 1975 following the Khmer Rouge victory. In early 1979, reverse migration began. Today, about one million Cambodians live in Phnom Penh.

STARTING AGAIN

War changed everything. So many men died during the years of war that women have taken over new areas of employment. Before the 1970s, a number of occupations—shopkeepers, village administrators, and government officials—were male bastions. War and revolution have transformed these patterns of employment, and today women have taken on a variety of new roles.

Men have also found their traditional patterns of employment affected by the years of turmoil and killing. Many jobs of a commercial nature—especially small trading businesses and shops—were traditionally the preserve of the Chinese and Vietnamese. These people suffered under Khmer Rouge rule, and many who were lucky enough to survive with their lives were anxious to leave the country after the Vietnamese pulled out in the early 1990s. Cambodian men, accustomed to thinking these were jobs beyond their ability, are now succeeding as small traders and shopkeepers.

A vacuum was also created by the virtual extermination of the country's

A DEADLY CHALLENGE

No other country in a state of peace has so many land mines threatening its civilian population every day. When a farmer is unfortunate enough to step on a land mine, the farmer's family can be reduced to poverty within days. A vehicle has to be hired to take him or her to the hospital, which can be 30 miles (48 km) or more away. Once there, the family has to pay for treatment and medicine. The total cost of the accident can add up to an entire year's income for a family.

It is estimated that seven million mines have been planted throughout the country—every month about 300 people step on mines. In Cambodia, about one in every 250 people is an amputee. Clearing a minefield is both a time-consuming and dangerous task.

middle-class professionals by the Khmer Rouge. When some semblance of order was restored by the Vietnamese invasion, there was a need to repopulate—literally—the capital of Phnom Penh. Many Khmers of rural descent, with little or no previous experience of city life, found themselves drawn into an urban lifestyle for the first time.

The United Nations organized the resettlement of over 250,000 people from six refugee camps in Thailand. About 5% of the population had fled to these camps over the years and they were shifted back to Cambodia in 1992 and 1993. The original terms offered to the refugees were very generous: they were allowed to choose their location and receive sufficient land to grow rice as well as the materials for building a house and the necessary farming and domestic tools to begin a new life.

Unfortunately, too many of the refugees chose to resettle in the Batdambang region because this was the most prosperous agricultural part of the country. There was not sufficient land to go around so the United Nations was forced to offer less attractive terms. Many refugees were persuaded to settle in other parts of the countryside or to move to towns where small businesses could be started. Instead of land, returnees were offered a cash payment of US$50.

Interpersonal relationships in Cambodian society are governed by rules of etiquette that are often quite formal. This acceptance and respect for hierarchy can be difficult for outsiders to understand.

The village home often houses three generations of a family, with a set of grandparents living with one of their grown children.

THE VILLAGE HOME

The typical home in the countryside is built by the family who lives in it. The general shape is rectangular and the floor is supported above the ground by wooden stilts. The space between the ground and the wooden floor is between five and 10 feet (1.5 to 3 meters), the actual size depending on the degree of flooding that is anticipated, as well as the prosperity of the home builders. Larger and stronger wooden piles are more expensive.

The roof is inexpensively thatched, using locally available leaves from palm trees or just dried savannah grass. Large protruding eaves are constructed as a means of keeping the walls dry during the monsoon rains. The walls themselves are put together by overlapping panels of timber or woven bamboo that are attached to the posts holding up the roof. At least one of the walls will have an open window space that is covered by a thick mat during heavy rainfall.

A typical hill tribe village has a character that is a little different from the usual Cambodian rural settlement. The village is laid out in a circular shape, with an outer ring of huts for married couples. Inside this circumference is a smaller ring of huts for unmarried women and village guests. In the center of the village, there is usually a communal long house where the elders gather for discussion and decision-making.

A COUNTRY DAY

A farming family rises at dawn, accompanied by the crowing of the cocks from beneath the house, where they share the living space with other fowl plus a pig or two and the household oxen.

After the family washes in a barrel of rain water with the aid of an opened coconut shell, breakfast is prepared and consumed. The husband then departs with his packed lunch for a day's work in the fields that are owned by his family. The children have their breakfast and prepare for a day at school, one that is likely to be run by Buddhist monks and which may well be situated near the local temple. Most children walk to school and then back again in the afternoon.

During the day, the woman of the house prepares food, feeds the farm animals, and washes the family clothes. At night the home is lit by an oil lamp. The family spends the evening together and retires early, before 10 p.m. The main interruptions to this pattern of life are occasioned by festivals and religious events at the local temple.

For most villagers, the marketplace is a focal point where they catch up on the latest happenings and news.

Most villages have a sala *("SAR-la"), or open pavilion, which is used for general meetings, or as a temporary shelter for visitors.*

THE FARMING YEAR

The annual farming cycle is broadly determined by the process of growing rice. The grains of rice that will be used for planting are dried in the sun. It is then necessary to prepare small dikes to carry the water that is so essential to the growth of the plant.

After the seeds sprout, they are transplanted by first gathering bundles of the stems and soaking them for two or three days in a corner of the field. Each seedling is then planted in the plowed mud. Oxen are used to plow and prepare the fields. Between the months of May and October, there is a constant need to remove the weeds, which would otherwise choke the growing rice.

The end of the rainy season—around October—is the time to harvest the rice. Farmers work together to help cut, tie, and thresh the crop. The threshing is done by hand, and the separated grain is carefully collected. The wasted stalks are gathered and later used as fertilizer for the soil. Each farm household keeps sufficient rice to feed itself for a year. The remainder is sold for cash to a government-run office.

Between early 1979 and 1989, rice farming was managed or controlled collectively by "solidarity groups." Each production team consisted of about 15 households and was responsible for working 24–36 acres (10–15 hectares) of land. After the Vietnamese withdrawal, rice farming reverted back to private and family-based production.

HILL TRIBE RHYTHMS

In the remote Ratanakiri province, over 200 miles (322 km) from the capital, some 80% of the population of 72,000 are hill tribe people. They are classified as Jarai, Krung, and Tampuan, and their lifestyle has continued unchanged for centuries. A slash and burn agriculture is supported by the farming of rice and the growing of a few vegetables. Water buffalo and cows are raised in small numbers.

The selling of surplus rice is the main way of raising cash. The possibility also exists of some dangerous mining work for semiprecious stones that are then sold to visiting Chinese or Khmer traders. Such work is dangerous because the caves are usually unexplored. It is not uncommon for miners to lose their way and become trapped, or to die from sudden rockfalls caused by primitive mining methods.

Most villagers in the remote northeast have no interest in politics. Names like Pol Pot and Norodom Sihanouk mean nothing to the typical hill tribe villager. Yet ironically, the province of Ratanakiri was one of the most heavily bombed provinces during the Vietnam War.

The Ho Chi Minh Trail passed through the region and was consequently carpet-bombed by Americans. In the early 1970s, Pol Pot located his main base in the province. For the pipesmoking hill tribes, though, national politics merit no attention. Working in the fields with a cane rucksack that carries the day's lunch is the normal pattern of life.

Folk medicine is still practiced in Cambodia, especially among the hill tribes. A common practice is to lubricate the skin covering the affected part of the body and rub it briskly with a copper token. The rubbing is done in a direction away from the head of the sick person. The theory is that the "bad" blood comes to the surface. The tokens used are usually family heirlooms.

Hunting is still the most popular means of providing food among hill tribes. The crossbow is the standard weapon to hunt wild boar or other animals, using poison-tipped bamboo arrows. A few villagers possess AK-47 assault rifles, which are also used for hunting.

An apartment block in Phnom Penh. The population of Phnom Penh and other urban areas fluctuates according to the season, with many farm workers seeking casual work in a largely informal economy.

URBAN LIFE

The capital city, Phnom Penh, is the only place in Cambodia where an urban lifestyle has firmly taken root. Phnom comes from the Khmer word for hill, while Penh was the name of a devout woman who, in the 18th century, had a small temple constructed on the summit.

The influence of the French is still evident in the broad tree-shaded avenues and old colonial buildings around the city. Recent investments by foreign companies have added some modernity to the place— advertisements for familiar consumer brand names now deck public places—and people, especially men, tend to dress in Western clothes. Compared to other capital cities, even those in other parts of Asia, the pace of life is never fast. The lifestyle of most urban dwellers remains a very calm and relaxed one.

HEALTH

The consequences of a complete breakdown of health services under Pol Pot can still be felt throughout Cambodia today, more than 15 years later. Only in the last few years has international aid filtered into the country.

The following figures summarize the difficult situation in Cambodia today:

- Life expectancy is just 49.7 years.
- The infant mortality rate is 120 per 1,000 live births (the average among Asian countries is 83).
- Only one out of every five children survives the first 12 months.
- The maternal mortality rate in childbirth is 25 per 1,000 live births.
- Only some 12% of the population in rural areas and 20% in urban areas have access to safe drinking water.

A village hospital in the countryside. There are some 34 hospitals in the country, with 506 doctors and public health officers under the Ministry of Health.

EDUCATION

The Khmer Rouge destroyed every textbook along with all school equipment and facilities. Education was condemned as corrupt; schools were replaced by indoctrination programs that sought to instil Pol Pot's ideology. Before 1975, there were about 20,000 teachers in Cambodia, but by 1979 there were only about 5,000 left. The rest had either died or fled the country.

There has been a massive effort in recent years to make up for lost time. The following statistics reveal some of the progress that has been made:

- There are now over 70,000 teachers.
- In 1990, 82% of school-age children were enrolled in primary school (91% in urban areas and 76% in rural areas).
- Adult literacy is estimated at 60–70%.

For years, succeeding in the educational system was one of the few alternatives to peasant life in Cambodia. Success in education meant gaining a diploma. This allowed the holder to obtain an administrative position in a sprawling bureaucracy that was based in the towns, but that extended its influence and control to the countryside as well.

As in other areas of Cambodian life, the ideology of the Khmer Rouge showed a radical rejection of conservative structures in the life of the country's citizens. Anyone with a diploma was condemned as an "intellectual" and sentenced to hard labor or even executed.

Young Cambodians lining up at the start of the school day. Primary education is compulsory for six years between the ages of 6 and 12.

THE ROLE OF WOMEN

When a woman marries she keeps her maiden name, an acknowledgement of the fact that she will not be losing her identity. Women have traditionally been regarded as active partners in a marriage. They bring up the children and run the home. They also take charge of the family's domestic budget and are responsible for the purchase of food.

The important role that women play in a marriage is reflected in the Cambodian proverb: "If you are a colonel, your wife is a general." Another telling reminder of the respect accorded to women lies in the fact that the family riches—in the form of precious stones—are in the personal care of women.

The riches may take the form of personal jewelry that is worn by the woman when she is not working in the fields or the house. Traditionally, the family jewels are kept wrapped up in a small bag and only brought out on special occasions.

The years under Pol Pot and the warfare that engulfed the country before and after this regime were extremely difficult ones for Cambodian women as well as men. As more and more men were killed and maimed, the women were left behind with sole responsibility for bringing up the children.

When Pol Pot emptied the towns of their entire populations and enforced a collective form of agriculture, women were often separated from their children.

In Cambodian society, both male and female children inherit equal shares of the family land from the parents.

63

WEDDINGS

Marriages are still often arranged, with the young woman having little chance to veto the choice. If a family were asked if they would force their children to marry, they would strenuously deny that this would happen because in theory, the young woman does have the right to refuse. In practice, because marriage often takes place soon after puberty, not many young girls challenge their parents' wishes.

Nevertheless, a woman has the right to terminate an unhappy marriage. Divorce is accepted and there is no stigma attached to it. However, the chances of a divorced woman or man remarrying is affected by their family's wealth, as well as their own personal qualities.

The civil marriage ceremony is not really a ceremony at all. It consists of little more than presenting to a local official the birth certificates of the bride and bridegroom and declaring their willingness to be registered as married. A traditional wedding, on the other hand, is an occasion for festivities. If the parents of the bride or bridegroom adhere to tradition, the day for the wedding is decided according to the horoscopes of the couple.

Whether in the countryside or the towns, weddings are a time for dancing and eating. In Phnom Penh, families who can afford to do so erect an awning in front of their house, with tables and chairs laid out on the pavement for guests. In the countryside, a temporary shed is often erected. The food is cooked outside in large pots over gas burners. Such street wedding parties are more likely to be held on a Sunday because this is when most people have a day off from work.

Small gifts are exchanged between the family members of the bride and bridegroom to celebrate the new family relationships that have been created by the marriage. Traditionally, a scarf is given by one or both parties to "fix the words and tie the hearts" of the newly married couple.

Opposite: **A newly-married couple. Wedding festivities may last up to three days, although this is now less common because people cannot afford to stop work for this length of time.**

RELIGION

FOR MANY CENTURIES, Buddhism was inextricably woven into the texture of Cambodian life. It was a vital part of the Cambodian's sense of cultural and national identity. Buddhism found its way into the daily pattern of people's lives and affected their lives on many different levels. It characterized and shaped their attitude to life on a philosophical level, while also, more practically, it determined the way they celebrated their holidays and provided opportunities for family reunions.

The overwhelming majority of Cambodians are Buddhists. Before the Khmer Rouge took over in 1975, there were over 3,000 monasteries in the country and more than 64,000 monks. Life in the countryside was closely bound to the local temple, and monks were highly respected figures.

Pol Pot's regime disbanded all the temples, and Buddhist monks became prime targets of persecution. The vast majority of the monks were executed or died from overwork and lack of food while being forced to work in the countryside. Perhaps as few as 2,000 monks survived the Pol Pot years of 1975–79.

According to Khmer Rouge ideology, Buddhism was merely a way of deceiving people. Pol Pot's minister for education declared in 1978 that "under the old regime, peasants believed in Buddhism, which the ruling class utilized as a propaganda instrument."

Attempting to wipe out all Buddhist beliefs and practices in one violent stroke was psychologically and culturally traumatic. The same minister for

Above and opposite: **Buddhist monks in their distinctive saffron robes are again becoming a familiar sight in Cambodian society today.**

Buddhist statues, made from cement, for sale. Most religious statues in Cambodia were destroyed during the Pol Pot years. When the Vietnamese invaded Cambodia in 1979, Buddhist delegations arrived in the country and temples once more opened.

education complacently declared that "with the development of revolutionary consciousness, the people stopped believing and the monks left the temples. The problem is gradually extinguished. Hence there is no problem." For the average Cambodian, however, this was a destabilizing shift.

Despite this horrific persecution, Buddhism was revived in 1979 with the help of Vietnamese monks who came to Cambodia and began to ordain new monks. Buddhism is once more finding its way back into Cambodian society, but the traumatic experience of turning temples—a cherished part of most Cambodians' lives—into pigsties and stables is difficult to measure.

BUDDHISM

Buddhism's roots lie in the teachings of Prince Gautama Siddhartha, which built upon and reacted against the then-prevailing beliefs of Hinduism.

Hinduism and Buddhism share a basic belief in the dynamic nature of existence. Birth and death are seen as the twin extremes of an ongoing and cyclical process that involves all forms of life—human and non-human. The fundamental beliefs of Buddhism appear to be deeply embedded in the Cambodian consciousness, considering the manner in which the religion has revived after its systematic elimination under the Khmer Rouge. Ironically, Pol Pot himself spent a number of years as a novice monk when he was a young man.

Buddhists believe that desire—and thus suffering—can be stopped by following the eight-fold path of right views, intention, speech, conduct, livelihood, effort, mindfulness, and concentration.

THE LANGUAGE OF BUDDHISM

Samsara ("sum-SA-ra") The endless cycle of death and rebirth. The word comes from Sanskrit and translates as "a wandering through." The term captures the Buddhist idea of life as one stage in a long journey.

Karma ("KAR-ma") The sum of a person's behavior in a previous existence, which is seen as determining the person's fate in a future life. In other words, how a person behaves and conducts their life today will result in an improved or impaired karma, which will eventually influence the nature of their future existence.

Nirvana ("ner-VAH-na") The final and perfect escape from karma, nirvana involves a loss of individuality. Nirvana comes from Sanskrit and means "extinction."

The Four Noble Truths are:
   1) Existence is suffering.
   2) Suffering is caused by desire.
   3) Conquer desire and suffering will cease.
   4) Follow the eight-fold path in order to conquer desire.

THE FOUNDER OF BUDDHISM

Prince Gautama Siddhartha was born into a wealthy, ruling family in what is now Nepal in the sixth century B.C. Around the age of 30, he gave up his life of luxury, left his wife and the court behind him, and renounced all earthly ambitions. For six years he practiced an extremely austere life, one bordering on enforced self-punishment.

Eventually he came to realize that the road to enlightenment lay not through such a life of denial, but through meditation. Legend records how he experienced enlightenment one day when he was sitting in meditation under a fig tree near Buddh Gaya, a village in India.

For the next four decades he led the life of a teacher, showing through example how to practice the good life that leads to enlightenment. He died at the age of 80, having influenced so many people that a new religion was in the process of being created.

Buddha means awakened or enlightened one. It is a title, not a proper name.

Buddhism has no belief in an omnipotent god. Neither is there a belief in a heaven after death. Both concepts relate to the idea of a beginning (god) and an end (heaven), but Buddhism is best understood in terms of a circle, rather than a straight line with a beginning and end point.

What this means for the individual believer is that one's present life is merely a stage in an ongoing progression. Death is seen as both the end of one stage of life and the beginning of another stage. Death is a transition point, an interchange on the subway of eternal life. The individual is reborn in a new form, and not always as a human. Eventually, it is hoped, the individual will progress and reach a final state of enlightenment known as nirvana.

SPREADING AND DIVIDING THE WORD

In the centuries following the Buddha's death, his teaching gradually spread across India. In the seventh and eighth centuries, the Buddha's beliefs were systematically persecuted within India and eventually stamped out by Islam. By then, it had been spread by monks to Ceylon (now Sri Lanka), Tibet, and most of Southeast Asia. In all these countries it is still an influential religion with millions of devout followers.

During the early period of Buddhism's growth, a major schism occurred because of different interpretations given to the philosophy. The disagreement has resulted in a permanent division of Buddhism into

A depiction of the Buddha in a temple painting. Images are important features of Buddhist temples, monasteries, and shrines. They generally show the Buddha meditating, teaching, or reclining. These represent his enlightenment, years of teaching, and passing to nirvana.

Mahayana and Hinayana.

The form of Buddhism that came to flourish in Cambodia was Hinayana—also known as Theravada, "the Way of the Elders." In the view of many scholars, this is regarded as probably the closest to the original teachings of the Buddha. The other form of Buddhism is found mostly in Tibet, Nepal, parts of China, Korea, and Japan.

Today, some young men spend as little as two weeks as novice monks in a Buddhist temple, compared to several months 25 years ago.

BECOMING A MONK

It is difficult to be sure about the total number of monks in Cambodia, partly because so many were killed by the Khmer Rouge and partly because becoming a monk is not like becoming a member of the clergy in, say, the Christian religion, where joining the clergy is usually considered a permanent vocation. Becoming a Buddhist monk, on the other hand, is something that most men hope to experience at some stage in their life. Only a few Cambodians decide to become monks for life. Most enter a temple for a few months or less, before returning to their normal working life.

A common practice is for a young man to take temporary Buddhist vows at some stage between leaving school and getting married. There is an ordination ceremony that is held before the beginning of Vassa, the monastic period of prayer that coincides with the rainy season. For the

A MONK'S DUTIES

There are a number of general rules that govern a monk's life. They can be expressed as a series of prohibitions against:
- The taking of life
- Stealing from others
- Behaving in an unvirtuous manner
- Telling falsehoods
- Drinking alcohol
- Using personal adornments
- Exciting the senses through dancing or singing
- Sleeping on a raised bed

Besides these broad prohibitions, there are 227 vows that a monk must follow.

duration of his spell as a novice monk, a young man leads a simple life based upon the Buddha's renunciation of wealth and luxury. As a result, the young man improves his karma and increases his spiritual worthiness. The immediate family of the young man also accrue spiritual merit and feel suitably proud when a close relative dons the orange robe.

In order to become a monk for life, a man must be a bachelor and over 21 years of age. It is assumed that he will have studied Buddhism for a number of years. The decision to enter a temple on a permanent basis is purely a personal decision. At any stage a monk can reconsider his decision and return to secular life.

Monks are once again becoming a common sight in Cambodia. Unlike Christian monks, their lives take them outside their monasteries on a daily basis. Traveling around with an alms bowl is part of their daily routine because monks do not receive a set salary. Instead, they rely on their local community for practical support.

Monks in Cambodia, like their counterparts in Sri Lanka and the rest of Southeast Asia, follow the Theravada school of Buddhism, which was codified during the first 500 years after the death of the Buddha.

WOMEN AND BUDDHISM

Women cannot become monks in the same way as men, but they are allowed to live in temples as lay nuns. Lay nuns wear white robes, and their heads are usually shaved. The rules governing their conduct are not as prescriptive as those applying to men. Consequently, they do not command the same level of social worth.

In the eyes of many, women who choose to reside in a temple to study Buddhism and meditate are often purer in their motives than their male counterparts. For young men, joining a temple as a novice monk is sometimes as much a social convention as a religious calling. There is also undoubted social esteem that accompanies the act of entering a monastery for most men.

This is not the case for women. Therefore, when a woman chooses to enter a temple, it is often because she is drawn to the teachings of Buddhism.

LIVING IN A TEMPLE

A temple complex—the Buddhist equivalent of a monastery—is composed of a small number of buildings enclosed by a wall with a main entrance. The main building is the temple itself, which contains the chief Buddha statue. There are also living quarters for the resident monks and a few open hall areas.

The daily routine for a Buddhist monk begins with an early morning period of meditation and prayer. This is followed by a walking journey in the neighborhood with the purpose of collecting food for the day. Traditionally, monks eat their one meal before noon and refrain from food for the remainder of the day.

A monk's primary purpose when living in a temple is the attainment of personal salvation by accruing good karma. As Buddhism does not subscribe to the belief in a supreme god, a temple is not like a church, where a member of the clergy conducts services for lay devotees. The nearest equivalents to a church service are the religious festivals, where monks and lay believers come together to celebrate their common sense of spirituality.

EVERYDAY BUDDHISM

Most Cambodians are Buddhists and are aware of their religion's equivalent of the Christian Ten Commandments. These general rules for good living prohibit the taking of life, stealing, committing adultery, drinking alcohol, and telling falsehoods.

The ordinary Cambodian is not striving to reach a state of nirvana—a highly mystical concept that is more an ideal than a practical goal. It would be more realistic to say that the ordinary Cambodian Buddhist is content to try and improve the quality of his or her spiritual life by accumulating merit in their present existence. Sufficient merit will improve their chances when it comes to rebirth. In this respect, at least, Buddhism bears some resemblance to the Christian idea that a person's behavior in this life will determine what happens to them in the next world.

A representation of the Buddha is found in most Cambodian homes and shops, usually in the form of a statue placed on a shelf or in a small alcove. Alongside this formal acknowledgement to Buddhism, there is also a widespread belief in ancestor worship and the existence of local spirits. It is not uncommon to see Cambodians wearing small charms, which are believed to protect them from unhelpful spirits. In the countryside especially, it is often thought that an illness might be due to the malign influence of a spirit. Treating an illness is often a combination of taking medicine and engaging in a folk magic that seeks to drive out evil spirits.

Temples offer Cambodian Buddhists a place to seek solace or spiritual guidance.

ISLAM

One of the main minority religions in Cambodia is Islam. The country's Muslims are mostly descended from the Chams, who came from what is now central Vietnam after the decisive defeat of the Champa kingdom by the Vietnamese in 1471.

Islam, together with Buddhism and Christianity, is one of the major religions of the world. It has an estimated one billion believers worldwide. The Middle East, where Islam was founded by the Prophet Mohammed in the seventh century, has traditionally been the stronghold of the religion. Sizable populations are also found in countries such as Indonesia, which is the world's largest Muslim country, India, Pakistan, Bangladesh, China, and the United States.

The Chams are devout Muslims. Many have performed the *hajj* ("HAHJ"), or pilgrimage to the holy city of Mecca, where the Ka'bah, or House of Allah, is sited. It is the duty of every Muslim to visit Mecca at least once in their life, unless prevented from doing so by reason of poverty or illness.

One interesting way in which Cambodian Islam has been influenced by the dominant religion of Buddhism lies in the manner devotees are called to prayer. Generally, across the Islamic world, the faithful are called to prayer by the official call of the *muezzin* ("moo-EZ-in") from the mosque. In Cambodia, however, the call is announced by the beating of a drum—just as in Buddhist pagodas.

Unfortunately, there is another parallel between Islam and Buddhism in Cambodia. Both religions were ruthlessly suppressed between 1975 and 1979, and members of the Cham Muslim community were executed as a matter of policy.

CHRISTIANITY

The Roman Catholic Church in Cambodia consists of the Apostolic Vicariate of Phnom Penh and the Apostolic Prefectures of Batdambang and Kampong Cham. In 1992, there were three Catholic priests working in Phnom Penh.

Cambodia has an estimated 12,000 Roman Catholics. Like Buddhism and Islam, Christianity was banned in 1975 by the Khmer Rouge. The right of Christians to meet to worship was only restored in 1990.

LANGUAGE

THE COMMON LANGUAGE of Cambodia is Khmer—known appropriately enough as Cambodian—the mother tongue of the Khmer people. The language belongs to a linguistic group known as Mon-Khmer. Although Mon-Khmer languages can be found throughout Southeast Asia, Khmer itself is a distinct national language.

Khmer helps to preserve the identity of a people who are surrounded by countries with different cultures. Khmer is recognized by scholars as an ancient language and is regarded by many as far older than Vietnamese or Thai. This is often felt as a source of pride by educated Cambodians.

LANGUAGE UNDER POL POT

Under Pol Pot, the written form of the language was systematically destroyed. Schools were closed down and writing was regarded as redundant in the agricultural society that was being imposed across the whole country. Books were routinely burned, not because they contained uncomfortable ideas but because they were books. By 1978, there were very few books to be found anywhere in Cambodia. Under Pol Pot, the National Library was converted to a stable. Today, nearly 20 years later, Cambodians are beginning to read and write once more.

Anyone identified as a journalist by the Khmer Rouge was executed. The consequences are still seen today in the relative shortage of newspapers.

Above: **Stone inscription from the Angkor era in a Banteay Srei temple.**

Opposite: **Two of the many advertising billboards that dot the streets of Phnom Penh today.**

MON-KHMER

Mon-Khmer is a generic term for a wide group of languages and dialects that are spoken by different cultures across Southeast Asia. Khmer, spoken by some 10 million Cambodians, is the most widely spoken Mon-Khmer language.

The next largest is the Mon language, which is shared by over a million peasants in Thailand and southern Myanmar (Burma). Altogether there are about 100 distinct languages and dialects that are recognized as sharing important characteristics of the Mon-Khmer group.

The usage of Mon-Khmer languages over such a wide area suggests that the different forms and dialects are descended from an ancient language that was once widely spoken in Southeast Asia.

THE KHMER LANGUAGE

The Khmer language has two styles of writing. One is an angular form, called *chrieng* ("KRU-ng"); the other is a rounded script, called *mul* ("MUL"), which is reserved for special decorative occasions. The written form can be traced back many centuries to the Indian influence on the country. Even if you are unable to understand or even pronounce any of the words, the Khmer script is a beautiful example of calligraphy. It is written from left to right with no space between words.

There is only a present tense in the language; a reference to the past or the future is made by adding a suitable word to the sentence. For example, the sense of "I cooked the food" is conveyed by saying "I cook the food yesterday" or "I cook the food already."

Unlike some Asian languages, there are no tones to the Khmer language. On the other hand, there are 23 vowel sounds (there are five in English) and 33 consonants.

The word for the Cambodian currency—the riel—is of Portuguese origin, a throwback to the trading links that were established in the 17th century when Portugal was a world power.

The spoken form of the language today incorporates a number of words of French, Vietnamese, and Chinese origin. A number of Cambodian words for numbers—for "thirty" and "forty," for instance—are derived from Chinese. Terms from the language of government, like the words for "police" and "field marshal," have their origin in the French of colonial rule.

The language of the Chinese, who were influential for so long in the commercial life of the country, has retained a strong presence. Many Cambodian words for the terms of weights and measures, for example, are Chinese in origin.

Khmer newspapers are not widely available outside Phnom Penh because of the difficulties of newspaper distribution.

ELEMENTARY KHMER

What follows can only provide a very approximate guide to the pronunciation of Khmer. Westerners find the language an especially difficult one to master, and Western linguists readily admit that it does present challenges. For example, there are eight different letters that correspond to sounds that register somewhere between the *t* and *d* sound of English. There are four distinct letters that can only be represented in English by the *ch* sound.

Numbers:

pee ("PEE")	two
bram ("BRAM")	five
bram-pee ("BRAM-PEE")	seven

Greetings:

joom ("JEWM") *reab* ("RE-a") *suor* ("SUE-o")	Hello
lear ("LEA") *heouy* ("HOY")	Goodbye
suom ("SUE-um") *tous* ("too")	Excuse me

Basics:

bat ("BAH") (used by men)	Yes
jas ("JAHS") (used by women)	Yes
suom ("SUE-um")	Please
ar ("R") *kun* ("KUN")	Thank you

LANGUAGE EQUALS THOUGHT

The language of a culture is inseparable from the pattern of life that makes up that culture. This is now a commonplace of anthropology, of which the classic example is the many different words that the Inuit (Eskimos) of Canada use for snow.

The same is true of the Cambodian language when naming rice. Simple distinctions like "steamed rice" and "boiled rice" appear as very crude in a language that has over 100 different words for different types of rice. A culture that is so very dependent on rice has quite naturally developed a language precise enough to account for all its varieties and shades of difference.

Another example of the preciseness with which a culture's language can respond to its circumstances relates to the fact that Cambodia is predominantly an agricultural society. There is, for instance, a word that means "a small animal tucking in its legs as it runs and turns at a sharp angle."

An example of the way language reflects society is the complex manner in which the Cambodian language allows a person to address another person. In English, it is possible to say "how do you do?" or "how are you?" to address any person. In Cambodian, there are a number of different words for "you" that depend on the social relationship that is seen to exist between the speaker and the person being addressed.

There is one class of words to address close family members, and even within this group there are different words for older relations—who are due more respect—and younger brothers or sisters. Addressing a monk has its own terms, and whenever a member of the royal family is being referred to, there are other special terms of address.

There are two different words for "yes," depending on whether a man or a woman is speaking. Under Pol Pot's regime, such distinctions were rigorously condemned as vestiges of a stratified class-based society and outlawed.

A young child buying ice-cream from a street vendor. The urban accent he picks up growing up in Phnom Penh will identify him as an urban dweller to Cambodians who live in the countryside.

ACCENTS

The Cambodian language has accent differences according to the ethnicity of the speaker. The language as spoken by Khmers is not identical in its pronunciation to that spoken by a member of a hill tribe in the remote northwest of the country. There are also noticeable differences between rural and urban accents. The word for mother is pronounced "may" in the countryside, while urban dwellers are more inclined to pronounce the word as "ma."

An account by a survivor of the Khmer Rouge years relates how she felt constantly endangered by the fact that she had been brought up in Phnom Penh. As a former resident of the capital, she knew that the Khmer Rouge would regard her as probably middle class and therefore an ideological enemy. One of the first steps she took to disguise her background was to change her accent and pronounce words in the manner of a country person.

OTHER LANGUAGES

The Cham people, who live in parts of both Cambodia and Vietnam, have their own language. It can still be found written in the traditional Indianized script, although this is becoming increasingly rare. A Romanized script introduced by the French is far more common today.

In Cambodia, most Chams have remained Muslims, unlike the Chams of Vietnam, who have adopted the religion and language of the Vietnamese. The Cambodian Chams' adherence to their religion helps preserve not only their separate cultural traditions but also their language. Although nearly all Chams speak fluent Cambodian, they have preserved their own language at home.

Various hill tribes also have their own languages, but these languages are becoming increasingly marginalized. Vietnamese is still spoken by ethnic Vietnamese in Cambodia, and the Chinese dialects of Mandarin and Teochew are spoken by Chinese residing in the country.

Vietnamese at Phnom Penh's riverfront. The Vietnamese language remains the chief form of communication among the Vietnamese today, even those whose ancestors came to Cambodia generations ago.

A student scanning the many wall advertisements offering English language classes. This street in Phnom Penh has been dubbed "English Street" by local residents.

ENGLISH AND FRENCH

For as long as Cambodia remained a French colony, the language of government and education was French. Even after the French left, there remained a tradition of speaking French among the urban elite. Fluency in the European language was a way for upper-class Cambodians to distinguish themselves from the majority. Even today, it is not unusual to come across educated Cambodians over the age of 50 who are fluent in French.

During the 1960s, partly due to the growing U.S. influence in the affairs of the country, English began to supplant French. Both languages were still spoken by the educated elite when Pol Pot's army took control of the country in 1975. At that time, both French and English were regarded as signs of a decadent and corrupt lifestyle; anyone speaking either language was liable to be executed.

Such prohibitions were removed by the Vietnamese in 1978, but there was little need to speak any language except Cambodian in the immediate years of reconstruction and renewal. In recent years, with the opening up of the country to development through foreign investment, there has been an explosion of interest in learning English. There is little interest in returning to French because French is not the language of international commerce. Instead, Phnom Penh has become a mecca for any Cambodian wanting to learn English. Increasingly, the learning of English has become associated with economic progress.

In July 1992, two English-language weekly newspapers were launched: the *Phnom Penh Post*, based in Bangkok, and the *Cambodia Times*, based in Kuala Lumpur.

The traditional form of greeting in Cambodia is to press one's palms together at chest level and bow.

FRENCH VERSUS ENGLISH

Neighboring Vietnam and Laos share with Cambodia a French colonial influence, but in the late 1980s both countries declared English to be their official second language.

In the 1990s, however, Cambodia's links with France were vigorously renewed, and after 1993, Prince Sihanouk—who was the last Cambodian monarch to serve under French control—attempted to make French the second language of his country.

Schools were instructed to reintroduce French and government bills were to be printed in both Khmer and French. By mid-1995, however, Cambodian students made their feelings known. Over 1,000 pupils staged a protest in Phnom Penh over the compulsory teaching of French instead of English. One of the country's two prime ministers, the son of Prince Sihanouk, supported their demands on the basis that English "is the most popular language in the region."

ARTS

SOME OF THE RICHEST and most enduring aspects of Cambodian culture are found in the country's forms of art. The architecture of Angkor is the most famous example and is so powerful an artistic legacy that the Khmer Rouge used it to rationalize their policies.

"If our people can build Angkor Wat, they can do anything," announced Pol Pot in 1979. Ironically, the Khmer Rouge then set about destroying the country's cultural traditions; anyone with any connection with the world of art was ruthlessly murdered.

The complex of temples and royal buildings at Angkor—built entirely of stone and brick—is the supreme achievement of Cambodian art. Most of the temples were not built to house worshippers, unlike Christian or Muslim religious buildings. The Khmers walked around outside or gathered for prayers in wooden buildings that were erected separately. The existing buildings of Angkor were never intended for occupation by humans, but only for use as religious shrines. Only the gods were permitted to live in buildings of stone or brick. The remains of various wooden buildings have been discovered close to the *wats* (temples). These were the homes that made up the city of Angkor.

Most of the temples were built as acts of devotion to the Hindu god Vishnu. Building work culminated with Jayavarman VII, who built the Angkor Thom complex. For centuries, at the height of the Angkor civilization, each Khmer king strove to outdo his predecessor in the height, size, and splendor of his temples, culminating in the massive structures of Angkor Wat and the Bayon.

Above: **Excavation work at the Terrace of the Leper King in Angkor Thom. The process of restoring Cambodia's cultural traditions is one of the many urgent tasks facing the country.**

Opposite: **Scenes from a temple carving. Temples were used as sheltered homes for images of the gods.**

The South Gate is one of four gateways that lead to the Bayon. When Jayavarman VII set out to create Angkor Thom, he had to raze the older work of his predecessors, as the site at Angkor had become choked with over three centuries of grandiose temple building.

ANGKOR THOM

The walled capital of Jayavarman VII was immense. It was surrounded by a moat 325 feet (100 meters) wide, in addition to a stone wall 26 feet (8 meters) high, with four imposing gateways that led to the Bayon. The Bayon is a pyramid temple with a tower 150 feet (45 meters) high, with four huge carved heads at the top, facing the four compass points.

Encircling the main tower were 51 smaller towers with heads pointing in various directions. When a French writer first visited Angkor in 1912, he described the shattering effect of discovering this sight:

"I looked up at the tree-covered towers which dwarfed me, when all of a sudden my blood curdled as I saw an enormous smile looking down on me, and then another smile on another wall, then three, then five, then 10, appearing in every direction."

There are conflicting theories about the religious significance of Angkor Thom's architecture. The sculptures have been variously interpreted as representing the Buddha, Brahma, Shiva, and King Jayavarman himself.

ANGKOR WAT

Angkor Wat is the best known temple of the complex. According to legend, Angkor Wat was built by Indra, the Lord of Heaven, who came down to earth. Historically, however, King Suryavarman II was the ruler who began the building program. A number of monarchs then followed his example.

Angkor Wat measures about 2,800 by 3,300 feet (850 by 1,000 meters) and contains a number of walled courtyards that encircle a central, five-towered building. The structure was built to represent Mount Meru, the sacred mountain regarded as the center of the world in the Hindu religion. The five towers symbolize the five peaks, the surrounding walls are the mountains, and the moat is the ocean at the end of the world.

The temple area is enclosed by a square moat, which is more than 3 miles (5 kilometers) long. The adjoining wall is famous for its bas-reliefs and four august gateways. The large ground area is divided by long stone paths that are linked by the four gates.

The gates, in turn, lead to the inner sanctum, which contains a representation of Vishnu, to whom the *wat* was dedicated. The most ceremonial of the gateways faces westward, and the approaching stoneway is decorated with *naga* ("nah-GAH," or snake) balustrades. On each side of the balustrades are two separate buildings, which are thought to have housed the capital's library of books and court documents.

The remains of Angkor Wat, which was Cambodia's capital between the ninth and 15th centuries, stand as one of the world's great architectural achievements. Historians believe Angkor Wat was intended as Suryavarman II's mortuary shrine because it is oriented toward the west (according to Cambodian mythology, the west is the direction in which the dead depart).

TA PROHM

Built as a Buddhist temple during the 12th century, Ta Prohm is one of the largest Khmer buildings of the Angkor era. It is different from both Angkor Wat and Angkor Thom in that it has been left as it was found over a century ago by French archaeologists.

Here, more than at any other Angkor site, the work of nature has literally woven its way into the artistic stonework. Roots of massive trees have grown into and under the stone, and jungle growth is found everywhere. The result is what many consider a completely novel work of art—one that integrates the unrehearsed world of nature and the artificially-crafted world of art.

RESTORING THE PAST

Angkor was deserted around 1430 when the monarchy moved farther south for security reasons. Angkor Wat gradually fell into decline, though

ANGKOR'S BAS-RELIEFS

A bas-relief is a sculpture or carving in which the figures project a little way from the background. The bas-reliefs of Angkor make up the most impressive carvings of the temple complex. They usually illustrate figures and stories from the *Ramayana* and other Hindu classics.

What fascinates scholars and tourists about the bas-reliefs is the unique window they open on aspects of life in Khmer society. Examples of the type of armor and weapons used by the military are preserved in stone. So too are peaceful scenes of citizens shopping in the market or gambling, through staged cockfights, or fishing in a river. Many of the scenes preserved in the bas-reliefs are still found in modern Cambodia, as well as in many other communities around the world. In many ways, gender roles have remain unchanged over the intervening centuries: young men are seen setting off in small groups on hunting trips, while their female peers visit hairdressers.

it was used as a Buddhist pilgrimage center for some time. Some 400 years later, French archaeologists began to excavate the site. The story begins with a French naturalist, Henri Mouhot, who accidentally came across the ruins in the early 1860s. They were mostly covered in overgrown vegetation. The local inhabitants did not think it possible that their ancestors could ever have built such an astonishing temple complex. They told Mouhot that a race of giant gods had constructed the site.

Serious restoration work began in the early 1990s. When Mouhot found the site, it had been left to nature for centuries and strangler figs had already caused damage. Roots and vines, having found their way into small cracks, had grown and split walls open. Today there is some debate about the extent to which this kind of damage should be interfered with.

The long period of neglect allowed profiteers to plunder some of the statues. They were smuggled out of the country and sold to private art collectors around the world. The Khmer Rouge, for example, dismembered some of the statues and sold off the parts for revenue. As a result, a number of the famous statues that can be seen today are decapitated.

Henri Mouhot once declared that Angkor was "grander than anything of Greece or Rome."

Above: **The Silver Pagoda was first built out of wood toward the end of the 19th century and then rebuilt by Prince Sihanouk in 1962.**

Opposite: **A piece of sculpture, damaged by the Khmer Rouge, from the Terrace of the Leper King at Angkor Thom. Sculpture remains as evidence of Cambodia's glorious past only because of stone's relative imperviousness to natural decay.**

THE SILVER PAGODA

The Silver Pagoda in Phnom Penh was preserved by the Khmer Rouge, although over half of the pagoda's contents were looted by the army. Despite this, the extraordinary overall effect remains undiminished.

The main staircase that leads up to the pagoda is made out of Italian marble. Inside, on a dais, a golden Buddha is seated. The Buddha contains nearly 10,000 diamonds and weighs about 200 pounds (90 kilograms). Flanking the golden Buddha are two smaller Buddhas, one bronze and one silver. Behind the golden figure sits another Buddha—made of marble—and a golden litter used to carry the king on coronation day. Twelve people are needed to carry the litter.

The pagoda's interior walls are decorated with priceless examples of Khmer art—over a score of small gold Buddhas and crafted masks covered with jewels that were used by court dancers. A huge mural depicts scenes from the *Ramayana*.

SCULPTURE

Sculpture is a characteristic Cambodian art form. Although the most famous examples are those found at Angkor Wat, the history of Cambodian sculpture goes back to pre-Angkorian times. The National Museum of Art in Phnom Penh is the main repository for the country's stone masterpieces, including rare examples from the Funan period—beginning in the fourth century—as well as the Angkor and post-Angkor periods. Most of the art that pre-dates the Angkorian period is Hindu-inspired. Angkor sculpture, which represents the supreme achievement of Khmer art and architecture, goes beyond the Hindu influence and blends motifs and techniques from Javanese art and Champa architecture.

One of the remarkable features of classical Khmer sculpture is its ability to represent realistic facial details. A stone face from the 10th century is recognizably that of a contemporary Cambodian, while conveying a religious sense of serenity and philosophic calm.

Khmer power peaked in the 12th century when Angkor Wat was erected. The temples and their sculptures, culminating in Angkor Wat, are a permanent testimony to Cambodia's powerful influence in Southeast Asia.

MOTIFS IN KHMER SCULPTURE

The *asparas* ("as-PAH-rahs," below left) represent the Angkor ideal of female beauty. They lived in heaven, where they were consorts of Khmer heroes. Asparas are nearly always portrayed wearing fine jewelry. The heads of the asparas have, unfortunately, become one of the most sought-after pieces of Angkor sculpture on the international black market. A large number of them have disappeared since 1975.

Nagas are sacred snakes, guardians of water supplies, that date back to Hindu mythology. The word *naga* is Sanskrit for snake. In Hindu myths, the naga coils beneath and supports Vishnu on the cosmic ocean. Khmer artists drew upon these myths as material for their architectural designs. At Angkor they are often found on stone balustrades.

The *garuda* ("gah-ROO-dah") is a mythical half-man and half-bird creature. Traditionally, it is the enemy of the nagas. For unknown reasons, it appears later in Khmer architecture than any other motif.

Singhas ("SING-ngahs," below right) are lions that feature in Angkor architecture as guardians of temples. Their characteristic lack of realistic features has been attributed to the fact that the sculptors had probably never seen real lions.

DANCE

The history of Cambodian dance goes back 1,000 years, with its origins in the Indian influence on the royal courts. The courts shaped and encouraged this cultural tradition. The form of the dance is characterized by extremely detailed attention to the most minute movements of the dancer. The exact angle at which an elbow is pointed or a head tilted is all-important to the overall meaning of the spectacle.

Women perform the main roles in the court dance, including all the male parts. The only exception is the character of the monkey, which is always played by a man.

The Cambodian dance form is gradually returning to the world stage today. Due to their association with royalty, nearly all members of the national dance troupe were murdered by the Khmer Rouge. One of the few survivors was Pol Pot's sister-in-law, Chea Samy.

Some members of the national dance troupe who escaped the Khmer Rouge fled to the United States, where they kept alive their classic art form. Today, dance troupes are once again rehearsing scenes from Indian myths like the *Ramayana*. Looking to the future as well as the past, a group of Cambodian-American dancers and teachers have developed an original work entitled *Tep Kanhaka*.

The story revolves around the dream of a king who is worshipping at a shrine. He dreams that the carved goddesses come alive and walk down to address and comfort him by uttering their assurance that his prayers have been heard and will be answered. The king had been praying for his country's future.

One of the survivors of the Khmer Rouge was Chleng Phong, who later became a minister of culture. He speaks endearingly of his country's dance: "For me, the classical Cambodian dance is the perfection of human artistic expression."

THE LORDS OF THE DANCE

In the summer of 1990, the Cambodian National Dance Company—of which only 17 members had survived from the original 200—toured Europe. The tour represented a celebration of a cultural rebirth.

One of the women who worked hard to resurrect the company of which she was once a proud member is Chea Samy. She returned to Phnom Penh in 1979 and within two years, reopened the School of Fine Art to train new recruits. Some 80% of her recruits were orphans, the victims of war.

As all previous documents and books relating to the dances had been destroyed, the new company has begun cataloguing and photographing the many hundreds of subtle steps and gestures of head, arm, foot, and hand that constitute the repertoire of Cambodian dance.

LITERATURE

Cambodian literature has two great epics: the *Poem of Angkor Wat*, from the early 17th century, and the *Ramakerti*, which dates from between the 16th and mid-18th centuries and has its origins in the seminal Indian epic, the *Ramayana*. The subject matter of the *Ramayana*—the life of Rama—also occurs in Cambodian dance-dramas and sculpture. It survives as living testimony to the influence of Indian art on Southeast Asia. The epics were oral in nature and depended for their success on storytelling sessions by professional groups who recited the tales.

Folk stories have figured in Cambodian culture throughout recorded history. From about the 18th century, this populist tradition began to be supplemented by verse fiction. A common inspiration was the *Jataka*, the various stories of previous lives of the Buddha. The most popular of these recounts the story of Prince Vesandar, an example of supreme charity.

During French colonial rule, printing was introduced to Cambodia and acted as the catalyst for the development of new literary forms. The first modern novel to be written in prose, as opposed to the usual verse form, was *Suphat*. It was written by Rim Kin (1911–59) and was published in 1938.

Under Pol Pot, literature ceased to have any meaningful role in the cultural life of the country. Books, fiction and nonfiction, were destroyed as a matter of principle, and any display of literary knowledge or interest was regarded as a form of heresy.

Present developments in the economic and social life of the country are likely to lead to a renewal of the country's literary heritage. It remains to be seen if artists can still anchor themselves in their traditional culture. The explosion of interest in the English language may work against and undermine conventional Cambodian literary forms.

Angkor Thom is perhaps the country's greatest literary work because of the large number of inscriptions on its temples.

LEISURE

THE WESTERN CONCEPT OF LEISURE is not easily transferable to contemporary Cambodia. The country is poor, and for many Cambodians, the struggle to recover from the years of war and deprivation is an enormous challenge. Taking time off to pursue leisure activities has little place in the pattern of many people's lives.

At the same time, Cambodians are a friendly and easygoing people. They like to be sociable and they like to enjoy their work. Hard work is thus carried out in a relaxed manner.

As religious beliefs stress the temporary nature of an earthly existence, the importance of spiritual contentment appears ingrained in the Cambodian's nature. This helps explain why visitors to the country are often astonished by the courage and optimism with which Cambodians are trying to rebuild their lives.

Among remote hill tribes, pipe smoking is a popular pastime, especially among young women.

Opposite and left: **The lack of proper sporting facilities or equipment is seldom an obstacle to Cambodian children looking for fun. An impromptu game of soccer, for example, can easily be organized on a empty parking lot.**

A group of young boys enjoying an afternoon swim in the Mekong River to beat the heat.

VISITING TIME

A visit to a temple for a festival is a popular leisure activity. It is an occasion for a family to put on their best clothes. If the festival is a particularly important one, the family may have saved some cloth for the making of new clothes.

The Water Festival in Phnom Penh is an especially popular event. People from outside the capital use the occasion to make a visit to the city and meet friends and relatives.

The capital city offers the promise of work, and many young Cambodians have left their villages and traveled long distances in the hope of securing employment in Phnom Penh. The Water Festival represents an occasion for families to visit their sons or daughters in the big city.

In the past, a traditional form of entertainment in the countryside was provided by traveling troupes of dancers, who were hired to perform at a local festival or a wedding. The government hopes to revive this form of entertainment.

Leading the way is the reestablished National Dance Company. In the past, local dance troupes often presented classic stories taken from Hindu epics like the *Ramayana*, with easily recognizable character types such as the beautiful princess or the intolerant father. These are now being brought back.

LEISURE IN THE CITIES

The only place in Cambodia where neon lights advertise the kind of leisure activities familiar to most Westerners—movie theaters, restaurants, night clubs—is the capital city of Phnom Penh. Watching movies has always been a popular pastime with city dwellers, not least because the price of a ticket is affordable.

Whereas Westerners typically relax in the evening by going out, Cambodians are more likely to spend their evenings talking over the day's events with friends and neighbors. A friendly conversation is considered a worthwhile activity in itself, and the local storyteller is always a valued member of any community.

Even in Phnom Penh, where the impact of television is beginning to be felt, most people still conduct their lives at a leisurely pace. Most offices and shops close for at least an hour (and often twice as long) for lunch. Cambodians enjoy socializing with friends and neighbors, and the work ethic, which is a strong characteristic of Cambodians, is not allowed to

Like many other people around the world, Cambodians love going to the movies.

intrude on the need to find time for other people's company.

Television, nonexistent less than two decades ago, has now found its way into the capital, where it functions as a sign of personal wealth and worldliness.

In the countryside, television has still to make an impact; radios are more common. Folk plays and shadow plays are beginning to make a comeback, reclaiming the following they once had in farming communities on festive occasions. The figures that are used in shadow plays are usually cut out of leather and painted in an exaggerated style to convey the characters' personalities.

Gambling has traditionally been a popular male pastime, although there are no official betting shops or state lotteries in Cambodia.

A casino in Phnom Penh. Games of chance always attract a big crowd of eager participants.

A trishaw driver takes a break from work, parking on the waterfront in Phnom Penh.

FOLK DANCE

There is a difference between court dancing and folk dancing. Court dancing is highly formalized and akin to ballet in some respects. The dancers practice long hours and strive to perfect classic movements and postures. Folk dancing is less formally structured and allows for improvisation arising from the interplay between the group of musicians and the team of dancers. Drums are usually used to establish a leading rhythm, and the dancers then weave their movements around this rhythm.

The more flexible and improvisational nature of folk dancing helps explain how it managed to survive the cultural nihilism of the Pol Pot regime. Court dancers were a relatively small group of professional, elite dancers, who were singled out for persecution by the Khmer Rouge. Being based in Phnom Penh made them especially vulnerable. Members of folk dance troupes were more likely to live in rural areas, and because they had a rural background, they were less likely to be identified as enemies of the new regime.

FESTIVALS

MANY OF CAMBODIA'S FESTIVALS are religious in nature. As such, they are based around the local temple, which becomes the focus of attention. Special ceremonies are conducted in temples, and many people come with offerings of food and money. As monks are discouraged from accepting cash directly, a box is placed near the temple's entrance for devotees to place their gifts.

Attending festivals and giving food to monks is a way of gaining merit in this world and increases the likelihood of a better next life. There is often an element of spirit worship on many of these occasions, despite the fact that they are usually Buddhist events. Each monastery has one local festival, known as a *Kathen* festival, which it holds each year. These are nearly always held after the rainy season.

Opposite: **Drummers help enliven celebrations at a monks' festival at Angkor Wat.**

Left: **Boat races, with gaily-dressed contestants and brightly-painted boats, are a common and popular feature at the annual Water Festival.**

TWO CALENDARS

The dates of most festivals in Cambodia are determined according to the Khmer lunar calendar. Thus the actual dates of festivals vary slightly from year to year, although a spring festival is always held in springtime and a winter one always takes place in the winter months.

The Western calendar is used by the government and the business community, but when it comes to calculating the time of a festival a more traditional calendar is employed. This calendar is of Indian origin and is basically lunar, although various corrections are periodically introduced to bring it in line with the solar yearly cycle.

Buddhist festivals are calculated according to the lunar calendar, which begins in the month of November or December. The Cambodian New Year's Day, however, is based on solar calculations and is celebrated in April. The traditional calendar divides the 12 months, alternately, into male and female ones. According to tradition, a wedding festival should take place only during the female months. Each month is divided in half and the days are numbered one to 15 or one to 14 (months have either 29 or 30 days). The first half of any month, when the moon is waxing, has the word *kaoet* ("COW-er")—meaning to be born—added to the number. The second half of a month is indicated by adding the word *roc* ("raw")—meaning to grow less.

By tradition, certain days of the week are considered more auspicious than others. Saturday, for instance, is often avoided as a day for holding a local temple festival because it is deemed a day when unhelpful spirits are allowed to wander the earth. Such belief is more likely to be found among older people, especially those living in remote rural areas. The average Cambodian living in Phnom Penh would prefer a festival was not held on a Saturday simply because this is another working day.

CALENDAR OF FESTIVALS

April *Chaul Chhnam* is the name of a three-day festival that usually occurs around the middle of the month. It is an important event and marks the beginning of the Cambodian New Year.

Visak Bauchea occurs later in the month and is a commemoration of the birth and enlightenment of the Buddha.

May *Chrat Prea Angkal* is an agricultural festival that marks the beginning of the rice-sowing season.

September *Prachum Ben* occurs towards the end of the month and marks a time when villagers pay homage to their ancestors. This is a ritual of Hindu origin and serves as a reminder of the influence of non-Buddhist spirit worship that can still be found across Cambodia.

The festival is conducted mainly through monasteries, with people bringing offerings in the mornings. During the evenings, talks and sermons are given by some of the monks.

Over a period of 15 days, people make offerings of balls of rice to their ancestors. It is believed that the King of the Land of the Dead permits spirits to visit their relatives on earth during this period. On the last day, the 15th, Cambodians make a special effort to be in the village where the ashes of their closest relatives rest. Special cakes are prepared and offered to the local temple.

October/November *Water Festival (Festival of the Reversing Current)* As the second name suggests, this festival marks the moment when the Tonle Sap River reverses its flow. The Tonle Sap lake fills with the floodwaters of the Mekong for five to six months. The Water Festival commemorates the emptying of the lake water back into the Mekong.

January/February *Tet* marks the Vietnamese and Chinese New Year and is celebrated by the ethnic Vietnamese and Chinese citizens of Cambodia. It is essentially a family event and has some similarities with Thanksgiving in the United States. It is a time to gather with one's family members in a spirit of joy and participate in celebratory meals.

Local monastery celebrations, known as Kathen *festivals, serve as a focus for community solidarity. Everyone in the neighborhood contributes to the success of the festival, by donating food or clothing for the monks. Those who can afford it give cash donations. Cambodia is still an extremely poor country, however, and very few people are able to make gifts in cash.*

THE NEW YEAR

The Cambodian New Year is the occasion for the most lively festival period across the whole country. It lasts at least three days and is one of the few times of the year when the majority of Cambodians take time off from work. On the last day of the old year, houses are traditionally cleaned from top to bottom and everything is made presentable for the new year.

On New Year's Day, many Cambodians pay a family visit to their local temple and pray for a good future. Another tradition, though no longer common, is the making of small sand hillocks around the temple grounds and inserting little home-made paper flags in them.

Children use the holiday to fly their kites. The kites, which are made by the children themselves, are carefully crafted out of spare cloth and trimmed pieces of bamboo. Vegetable dyes are used to paint geometric designs or colorful animal shapes on the cloth.

Inexpensive fireworks, usually imported from China, also form part of the New Year celebrations.

BANNING FESTIVALS

Under Pol Pot, most of the traditional festivals were strenuously outlawed. All festivals were fiercely rejected by the Khmer Rouge, partly because they were often religious in nature and partly because some of them were associated with royalty.

For example, the agricultural festival that celebrates the beginning of the sowing season in May used to include a member of the royal family ritually plowing the first furrow of the year. The Water Festival involved a member of royalty officially commanding the waters of the Tonle Sap River to change their direction.

The only internationally-celebrated holiday that Cambodia observes with the rest of the world is Labor Day, or Workers' Day, on May 1.

MONK ORDINATION

The beginning of the rainy season is the traditional time for the ordination of monks and novices. The ceremonies, though highly rule-governed, are colorful social occasions. The young novices form a procession that winds its way around the ordination area three times.

The procession also includes a number of monks whose chanting provides the musical background to the ritual. Parents, friends, and relatives are understandably proud of the young men who are about to enter temple life, and they turn up in their best clothes to witness the event.

NATIONAL HOLIDAYS OF CAMBODIA

National Day	January 7
New Year	April
Victory over American Imperialism Day	April 17
Labor Day	May 1
Day of Hatred	May 20
Feast of the Ancestors	September 22

FOOD

FOR MUCH OF THE PAST 25 YEARS, Cambodians have been deprived of a normal, peaceful existence. In a period of four years between 1975 and 1979, an estimated one in seven Cambodians died from starvation or illness brought about by an overambitious and unsuccessful program designed to increase the country's rice production. The political changes in the 1990s have brought about better times for most Cambodians. However, malnutrition remains a problem in parts of Cambodia even today.

Cambodian food bears many similarities to food in other Southeast Asian countries. Rice, for example, is the staple diet of the people. For several years in the late 1960s, Cambodia was the seventh leading exporter of rice in the world. Fish is easily obtainable from the country's many rivers, the Tonle Sap, and the Gulf of Thailand and is the main source of animal protein for Cambodians.

Opposite: **Coconut cakes and other snacks for sale in a bustling Phnom Penh market.**

Left: **An elderly food vendor patiently awaits customers.**

Food stall helpers in Phnom Penh preparing tub-loads of rice for the evening meal.

RICE WITH EVERYTHING

Sii bay ("SEE-bay")—the Cambodian verb that means to eat—becomes "to eat rice" when translated literally. This is testimony to the importance of rice in the Cambodian diet. Only in exceptional circumstances would someone go through a day without having a meal that includes rice. It is the primary carbohydrate and energy source for Cambodians. The Cambodian liking for rice is not unusual in Southeast Asia. Their neighbors, the Vietnamese, Thais, and Laotians, share this dietary dependence.

Rice is the main but not the only feature of Cambodian food common to Southeast Asia. Many of the herbs and spices used to flavor dishes are found throughout the region. There is also a liking for the hot and sour tastes characteristic of Thai cooking.

The typical dish that accompanies a bowl of rice is fish. A fish-based soup is also commonly consumed with a meal, but the soup is not regarded as a separate dish that precedes the main meal. It is dipped into when the rice and fish are being eaten and helps to balance the dryness of the rice.

Meat, when available, is also eaten with rice. Chicken is the most common, followed by beef and pork. Wild game is not commonly available in urban areas, but in the countryside villagers like to supplement their diet with protein-rich wild boar meat or large birds, which are trapped.

A rice-based dish that is especially popular with Cambodians is called *an sam chruk* ("an-sam-KRU"). This meal is made by mixing pork that has been cut into tiny pieces with tofu and rolling the mixture in rice. Legend has it that a meatless version of *an sam chruk* was a personal favorite of the Buddha himself.

The most common kitchen utensil in Cambodia is the wok, a bowl-shaped frying pan that is used for cooking almost every meal.

AN SAM CHRUK (PORK BALLS)

¹/₂ lb (225 g) pork
2 small blocks tofu
2 cups rice
garlic

Cook 2 cups of rice according to package directions and keep it warm while you prepare the pork. Cut the pork into small pieces. Add some crushed garlic and fry in about 2 tablespoons of oil in a wok for about 2 minutes. Add the tofu, also broken into small pieces, and cook for another minute, stirring constantly. Add the pork and tofu to the rice and mix together into small balls. Serve hot with a cold salad.

FISH

Like rice, fish dominates the typical Cambodian meal. Depending on the season and where they live, Cambodians eat either fresh fish or salted, dried fish. Freshwater fish is mostly caught from the Tonle Sap or the Mekong River.

In recent years, however, the destruction of forests in many lowland central provinces has disrupted or destroyed natural breeding habitats of many species of freshwater fish.

When fresh fish is available, most Cambodians prefer to grill rather than boil or bake it. A traditional method of presenting food on a plate is to cut the grilled fish into small pieces and wrap them in leaves of lettuce or spinach. Additional flavor is provided by a fish sauce called *tuk try* ("TOUK-tra").

Top and above: **Dried fish displayed prominently to attract customers.**

CONDIMENTS AND SALADS

Fermented fish sauce, *tuk try,* is the most characteristic condiment in Cambodia. It has a distinctive odor, which those who are unused to the smell often find difficult to appreciate. *Tuk try* is made by fermenting salted fish in large pots for at least three months. This condiment is also found in Vietnam, but the Cambodian version is distinguished by the addition of ground peanuts.

Cambodian salads are different from those in the United States or Europe. They usually contain some meat, if available, and are flavored with herbs such as lemon grass, mint, and coriander. The result is a hot, spicy taste that has little in common with the typical cold salad of Western dinner tables.

Dried fish and rice—whether steamed, boiled, or fried—can become monotonously familiar and nondescript to the taste buds. Cambodians often enliven the taste of the basic ingredients with chilies and garlic. Various herbs are also added whenever they are available.

A vegetable market in Phnom Penh. Herbs, such as mint, are sometimes used in Cambodian cooking. In the countryside, wild herbs, known only by their Cambodian names, are also used.

117

SPECIAL MEALS

On special occasions, such as a wedding or an important festival like the New Year, the usual rice and dried fish meal gives way to something more elaborate. Fresh shrimp barbecued over an small open fire is a particular favorite with many Cambodians. So too are roasted sunflower seeds. Other delicacies include duck eggs, known as *pong tea kon* ("PONG-tee-ko"), which are eaten just before they are ready to hatch, and fried crunchy cicadas, known as *chong roet* ("CHONG-rot").

Another specialty consists of pieces of banana wrapped inside balls of sticky rice. A favorite desert for special occasions is jackfruit, which is used to make a pudding known as *sangkcha khnor* ("SANK-cha kor").

The French colonial era brought a different style of cooking to the

One of the many varieties of food that can be found at the Phnom Penh central market—insects. Fried, they become a favorite delicacy for Cambodians.

country, and there is still some tangible evidence of this. This is particularly the case when it comes to French bread. French cuisine, however, never reached the vast majority of rural Cambodians; it is mainly only in Phnom Penh that French influence is seen. Frog's legs are considered a local delicacy, but this predates the arrival of the French.

DRINKS

Cambodians enjoy drinking tea between—and often with—all their meals. Coffee is also drunk, either black or with condensed milk. Milk is rarely drunk by itself and is never added to tea. A visitor coming into a Cambodian home is more likely to be offered a cup of tea than any other refreshment.

In drink stalls in towns and Phnom Penh, the most popular cool drink is soda water with fresh lemon. A large slice of lemon is often placed on a side plate and the customer squeezes the juice into the water. Well-known international brands of canned soft drinks have also begun to appear in the capital. Cambodians generally do not drink alcohol.

119

A simple meal at a market stall is the Cambodian equivalent of U.S. fast food.

TABLE MANNERS

Rice, the basic component of any meal, is often placed on the table in a large serving bowl or plate. Each diner then fills their smaller individual bowl, refilling it later if they wish. Depending on how large or elaborate the meal is, there are serving plates for the fish and other dishes, and smaller, saucer-like plates for the condiments.

Diners use their chopsticks to add a quantity of the fish, meat, or vegetables to their bowl of rice. The bowl is typically held close to the mouth and the food eaten with the chopsticks. It is not uncommon, in rural areas especially, for people to eat an informal meal using just their hands instead of chopsticks.

When a meal is over, the chopsticks are placed across the bowl or just left by the side. Leaving the chopsticks sticking up out of the rice is considered bad manners.

THE POLITICS OF FOOD

The Batdambang region has traditionally provided Cambodia with most of its rice. There was a time before the 1970s when Batdambang provided all the rice that Cambodia needed, and the produce from other parts of the country could be exported. The fact that rice was the country's largest source of foreign exchange formed the basis for the economic policies of the Khmer Rouge, which emphasized the development of agriculture.

The Khmer Rouge planned to dramatically increase the country's rice production. The foreign currency earned would finance imports of farm machinery and fertilizer, and thereby help make the country self-sufficient. The government slogan was "three tons [of harvested rice] per hectare." This meant tripling the average yield throughout the country, with only four years allowed to achieve this miracle. The plan, however, ignored the facts: Cambodia was just emerging from five devastating years of war and there was a shortage of tools, seed, and livestock.

What followed was a desperate attempt to meet unreasonable quotas. Towns and cities were emptied of their population. The result was the deaths of hundreds of thousands of Cambodians from overwork and starvation. Today, Cambodia is still recovering from this traumatic period. The people of Cambodia remain the poorest in Southeast Asia, and for many families, malnutrition is just one bad harvest away.

Cambodians arriving by foot and in oxcarts for a rice distribution exercise in 1980.

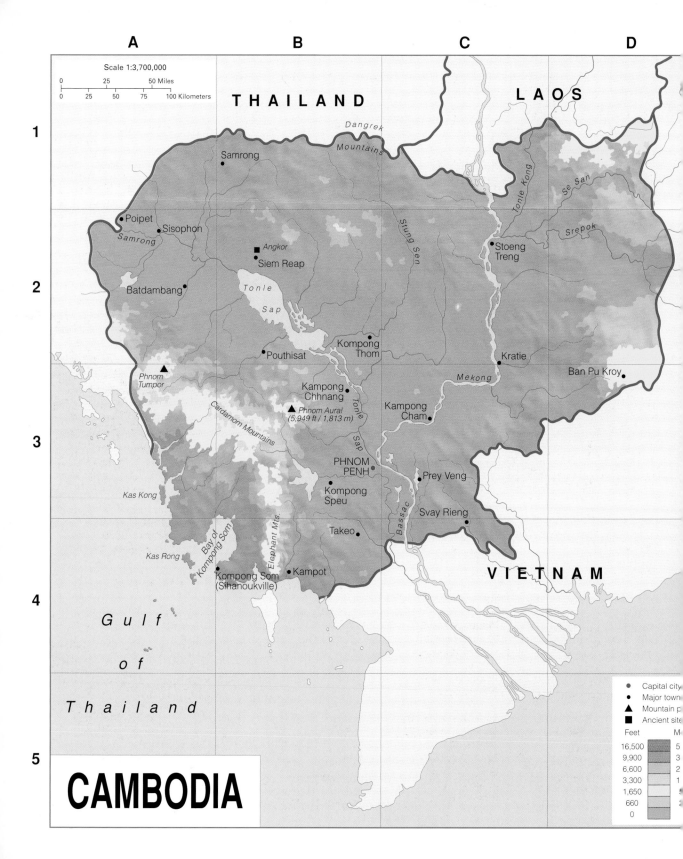

THAILAND

LAOS

A   B   C   D

Scale 1:3,700,000

0   25   50 Miles

0   25   50   75   100 Kilometers

1

Dangrek
Mountains

• Samrong

• Poipet

• Sisophon

Samrong

■ *Angkor*
• Siem Reap

Stung Sen

Tonle Kong

Se San

• Stoeng
Treng

Srepok

2

• Batdambang

Tonle

Sap

• Kompong
Thom

• Kratie

• Ban Pu Kroy

• Pouthisat

▲
*Phnom
Tumpor*

Cardamom Mountains

• Kampong
Chhnang

▲ *Phnom Aural*
(5,949 ft / 1,813 m)

Tonle

• Kampong
Cham

Mekong

3

Kas Kong

Sap

**PHNOM
PENH** •

• Kompong
Speu

• Prey Veng

Bassac

• Svay Rieng

• Takeo

Elephant Mts.

*Bay of
Kompong Som*

Kas Rong

• Kompong Som
(Sihanoukville)

• Kampot

VIETNAM

4

Gulf

of

Thailand

5

CAMBODIA

• Capital city
• Major town
▲ Mountain p
■ Ancient site

Feet   M
16,500   5
9,900   3
6,600   2
3,300   1
1,650   5
660   2
0

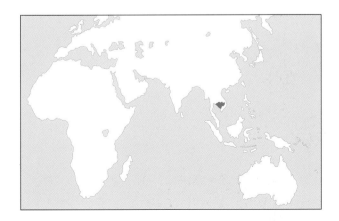

QUICK NOTES

AREA
69,898 square miles (181,035 square kilometers)

POPULATION
9.3 million (1993 estimate)

CAPITAL
Phnom Penh

OFFICIAL NAME
Kingdom of Cambodia

MAJOR LANGUAGES
Khmer (official language)
French

HIGHEST POINT
Phnom Aural (5,949 feet /1,813 meters)

MAJOR LAKE
Tonle Sap

MAJOR RELIGION
Theravada Buddhism

MAJOR RIVER
Mekong

NATIONAL SYMBOL
The sugar palm tree

NATIONAL ANTHEM
"Jham Kraham Cral" (Bright Red Blood Was Spilt)

MAJOR CITIES
Batdambang, Kampong Cham, Kompong Som, Kampong Chhnang, Kampot, Pouthisat, Kompong Thom

NATIONAL FLAG
Three bands—dark blue, red, and dark blue—with a stylized representation (in white) of the temple of Angkor Wat, with three towers, in the center

CURRENCY
1 riel = 100 sen
US$1 = 2,583 riels

MAIN EXPORTS
Rubber, timber, corn, soybeans, sesame, tobacco

POLITICAL LEADERS
Jayavarman II: founder of the Angkor empire in 802
Suryavarman II: king 1113–1150
Jayavarman VII: king 1181–1201
Norodom Sihanouk: king 1941–1955; recrowned king in 1993
Pol Pot: Khmer Rouge leader; premier 1976–1979
Prince Norodom Ranariddh: first prime minister 1993–present
Hun Sen: second prime minister 1993–present

ANNIVERSARIES
Day of Hatred (May 20)
National Day (January 7)

GLOSSARY

an sam chruk ("an-sam-KRU")
A rice-based dish made with tofu and pork, popular with Cambodians.

aspara ("as-PAH-rah")
One of four motifs common in Khmer sculpture. They are mythical consorts of heavenly heroes, and represent the ideal form of beauty.

chong roet ("CHONG-rot")
Cicadas fried until crunchy—a favorite Cambodian delicacy.

chrieng ("KRU-ng")
Angular form of the Khmer script in everyday use.

garuda ("gah-ROO-dah")
Mythical half-man, half-bird creature found in Khmer architecture.

hajj ("HAHJ")
Pilgrimage to Mecca. One of the five pillars of Islam.

karma
The sum of a person's actions in a previous life, which determines his or her fate in a future life.

kaoet ("COW-er")
Word, meaning to be born, that is added to the number in the first half of a month.

muezzin ("moo-EZ-in")
The mosque official who makes the call to prayer.

mul ("MUL")
Rounded script of Khmer language used for special decorative purposes.

nirvana
The final and perfect escape from karma that involves loss of individuality.

naga ("nah-GAH")
Sacred snakes from Hindu mythology that act as guardians of water supplies.

pong tea kon ("PONG-tee-ko")
Duck eggs, which are eaten just before they are ready to hatch.

roc ("raw")
Word, meaning to grow less, that is added to the number in the second half of a month.

samsara ("sum-SA-ra")
The endless cycle of birth and rebirth in Buddhism.

sangkcha khnor ("SANK-cha kor")
Jackfruit pudding.

sarong ("sah-RONG")
Dress worn by Khmers and Chams, typically knotted at the waist.

sii bay ("SEE-bay")
Cambodian verb meaning to eat. Translated literally, it means "to eat rice."

singha ("SING-ngah")
Mythical lions in Khmer architecture that act as guardians of temples.

tuk try ("TOUK-tra")
Fish sauce made by fermenting salted fish in large pots for three months or more.

wat ("wat")
Temple.

BIBLIOGRAPHY

Chandler, David P. *A History of Cambodia.* Boulder: Westview Press, 1992.

Chandler, David P. *The Land and People of Cambodia.* New York: HarperCollins, 1991.

Graff, Nancy Price. *Where the River Runs: A Portrait of a Refugee Family.* Boston: Little, Brown, 1993.

Greenblatt, Miriam. *Cambodia.* Chicago: Children's Press, 1995.

Ross, Russell, ed. *Cambodia: A Country Study.* Washington, D.C.: U.S. Government Printing Office, 1990.

Sam, Sien. *In the Land of the Red Prince.* New York: Vantage Press, 1994.

INDEX

INDEX

INDEX

PICTURE CREDITS